...una to Jeanine Basi...   *...em.*

Acknowledgements

Thanks and a tip of the sombrero to Michael Goldfarb, Gianni Palermo, Steve Berman, Paul Duncan, Richard Slotkin, Ion Mills, Alessandra Barbareschi, John Harvey, Steve Holland, Joel Finler, Mikey Carter, Mike Mewshaw, Clive Russell, Pat Butcher and Fran Michelman.

CONTENTS

Sergio Leone: The Western Landscape

I could whistle you the first eight notes of the theme from *The Good, The Bad And The Ugly*, and you would know instantly what I was talking about, with the same sort of certainty that comes with the music from *Gone With The Wind* (1939) or *Jaws* (1975) or *The Godfather* (1972). Yet the films of Sergio Leone continue to occupy a strange place in the foundations of the cinematic pantheon. In some circles, Leone is looked upon as a pulp-meister supreme, who could refine genre film-making to its essence. In others he's a flashy maker of B-movies, who used cinematic tricks and cheap violence to win an audience, and then gave into cinematic pretensions and lost his edge. To some, he's a creative genius of the first rank who could do no wrong. There is a grain of truth to all those positions, though I would deny the flash and assume that no film-maker can do no wrong, but those truths are part of the reason why Leone is such a fascinating film-maker.

Having watched and rewatched Leone's films, to me the most obvious point is that they are consistently entertaining; even after repeated viewing, they retain their basic power. Leone liked to say his films were fairy tales for adults, and they have that fairy-tale satisfaction which leaves the audience quoting lines, quoting favourite moments, quoting musical themes, a quality which is shared by both classic and cult films. Leone's films demand to be considered in both categories.

I propose to look at Leone primarily through the genre that made him famous, the Western, and also from the more specifically American context of that genre. I think this approach is both justified and important, because although foreign film-makers have had strong influences on American genre movies (the French New Wave, for instance, taking American gangster movies and recycling them into films that then influenced gangster films like *Bonnie And Clyde* (1967), or Akira Kurosawa borrowing from John Ford for *The Seven Samurai* (1954) which was then 'remade' as *The Magnificent Seven* (1960)) and, indeed, many of Hollywood's greatest genre movies were made by foreigners, Leone may be the first foreigner to create, within his own national context, an American genre which became a hit in America.

Leone's context included the American Western, because he was both a lover of the genre and a keen student of it. But if the influence of

American film was tempered somewhat by Leone's experiences of working with American film-makers in the 1950s, it was also enhanced by his own background as, literally, a child of the Italian film industry.

The early greats of the Western film were invariably people whose storytelling sensibilities were formed by 19th-century literature and values, both American and European. They grew up within the world of film-making, in the sense that they discovered the ways and means of filmic storytelling as they made movie after movie with ever-improving equipment. They also had immediate contact with the 'real' West, and not only because many early stars and stuntmen were ex-cowboys. Director Raoul Walsh played Pancho Villa in a film made with Villa's cooperation; Wyatt Earp was a frequent visitor to John Ford's sets.

When Leone began directing, those greats were approaching the end of their careers, yet Leone had the experience of actually working with Walsh, and with Ford's stunt director, Yakima Canutt. His overall experience of working with Americans was very much mixed, but some of the disillusionment he felt would be reflected in the unique and very personal style he would develop. In fact, it helped him to deflate and reconstruct the myths of the American Western.

The elements of Leone's style, which were formed in his Western films, remain with us today. Before we look at the man and his movies, it's worth asking ourselves: What are the elements that define Leone's work? Why do we still feel a tingle every time the guitar strings twang and the trumpet sounds and the steely eyes stare each other down?

The Lonely Anti-Heroes: In his *Studies In Classic American Literature,* DH Lawrence, writing about the original American frontier hero Natty Bumppo (aka Hawkeye, Deerslayer and Pathfinder) wrote 'the essential American soul is hard, isolate, stoic, and a killer. It has never yet melted.' As a description of The Man With No Name, this would take some topping. Leone created a character that refined the essence of the cowboy hero. It was a refinement which sprang from his perception of both the myths as he had seen them in American popular culture, movies and comic books, and the real Americans he had encountered - first the soldiers who marched through Italy during the war, and later the film-makers with whom he worked as a second unit director.

The Hollywood Western hero was defined by two things: his essential goodness and his quickness with the gun. Leone wondered why these two characteristics should be assumed to go together. Why should the hero always be the faster man? Would not, in a strange Darwinian sense, the faster man be the only one left who could apply for the role of hero? Leone's hero is defined, at least in part, by his refusal to wear the white hat of the classic Western. He is motivated by greed, by self-interest, by revenge, and by a narrow and sometimes psychopathic personal code that demands his self-image be protected. He may be differentiated from the truly evil villain, but his purpose is not necessarily to eliminate that villain, unless there is profit to be made. But he will be drawn, inevitably, to him, and just as inevitably, a confrontation will occur. Thus the familiar triangular relationship of Leone's protagonists develops, within which the borders between hero and villain begin to blur. His hero is not automatically the 'good guy' nor is his villain automatically the 'bad guy'; if you don't learn this from *The Good, The Bad And The Ugly* you never will.

The Italian Way Of Death: Since the showdowns between individuals who are drawn to each other because of their skill at killing are inevitable, in the end all that matters is who lives and who dies. Leone's characters become the very embodiments of death, to the point where it sometimes becomes difficult to tell who is dead and who is alive. Starting with the corpse Joe encounters riding out of San Miguel at the start of *A Fistful Of Dollars*, life and death are often interchangeable (think of the two corpses Joe leaves for Ramon to 'kill' later in *A Fistful Of Dollars*). This is the existential dilemma at the centre of Leone's final film, *Once Upon A Time In America,* where Noodles experiences death in life, and Max gets new life in death.

This Is A Man's World: These kinds of heroes must remain isolated from society; they will not wear a badge or defend civilisation. They function in a universe almost totally devoid of women; without the wives or mothers who symbolise civilisation in Hollywood's classic Westerns, who provide the civilising dance sequences for John Ford and dozens of others. Nor are there the whores of Sam Peckinpah's West. In Leone's Westerns, there are really only three women of significance. In *A Fistful Of Dollars,* there is Marisol, who is both Madonna and whore (albeit against her will) and Consuela Baxter, who is the real power in the clan, and in *Once Upon A Time In The West* there is Claudia Cardinale as Jill McBain, a whore turned into the ultimate civilising icon, whose burgeoning town literally pushes Harmonica and Cheyenne away. For these men to function, they need a stage on which they can play.

The Setting: Eternal Borderlands: We can instantly visualise a Leone Western through its setting; Leone's Spanish locations became as recognisable as Ford's Monument Valley. But he used them to a much different purpose. Leone's West is set on the fringes of the American frontier, in what is supposed to be the Mexican border area, not the prairies and mountains which pioneers cross. When he finally moves to Monument Valley for *Once Upon A Time In The West,* he uses the landscape in which Ford isolated groups of people forming their own society, in order to provide a stage on which his isolated individuals could perform. Leone's West is a stage, an arena, a chessboard, a tabula almost rasa on which the main players play. It is an empty landscape, which never becomes a character itself, as it might in Ford or in the Westerns of Anthony Mann. His towns are minimal and often empty of people (usually because they see his heroes, and thus trouble, coming and get out of the way). Not until the final scenes of *Once Upon A Time In The West* will we get any sense of civilisation's hordes flocking westward. Townspeople in Leone's film exist to play specific roles: in *A Fistful Of Dollars* we have a cantina owner, a bell-ringer and a coffin-maker, and that is it. In the films that follow we will see a 'civilian' only if his presence is necessary. Sheriffs and other lawmen are almost non-existent: in *A Fistful Of Dollars* one of the Baxters is also sheriff, and Eastwood ignores him; he takes the badge from a corrupt sheriff at the start of *The Good, The Bad And The Ugly*.

Indians play no part in Leone's West. His is not the story of manifest destiny sweeping aside, for better or worse, the natives who get in its way. His West is where the northern European gringos and the southern European Mexicans mix, impervious to the growth of civilisations around them (this will be challenged when Sean drags Juan into the Mexican revolution in *Duck, You Sucker)*. They seek only the space in which to find their fortunes and enact their rituals of violence. The only variation on this theme comes in *Once Upon A Time In The West,* where the railroad will bring civilisation behind it (although the crews we see doing the bringing, working on the track, are a veritable United Nations of America's not-yet assimilated!), and the conflicts are between gringos. However Harmonica, as revealed in the flashback scenes, is actually a Latino himself. Using isolate heroes interacting in a bleak landscape allows the viewer's interest to be directed directly at the characters and the way they relate to each other…

Visual Style: Up Close & Personal: When they first appear in the landscape, Leone's characters are defined by their appearance—their costumes, their cleanliness, their equipment all reveal aspects of their natures. Colonel Mortimer's arsenal of high-tech weaponry contrasts with Indio's holster worn Indio-syncratically across his shoulder, just as Tuco will later wear his gun hanging from a rope, as he himself is repeatedly hung.

But we really learn about the characters from Leone's use of close-up, not just of faces, but of their elements, and particularly eyes. It isn't simply the extreme nature of the close-up that pulls us into the essence of the duelling gunfighter, but the inordinate length of time for which those close-ups are held.

The Hollywood gunfight generally culminated in a walk, with the two protagonists moving toward each other. To understand what Leone does, think of the walk Gary Cooper makes in *High Noon* (1952), and the way director Fred Zinnemann cuts to shots of his boots walking down the street to emphasise the inevitability of the action he is moving toward. A few years later, in *Forty Guns* (1957), Samuel Fuller will show us Barry Sullivan's boots in similar fashion, as he walks down John Ericson, and he will also give us an extreme close up, in widescreen, of Sullivan's eyes. He doesn't linger, but the effect is there.

In those Hollywood shoot-outs, the streets of the town are the setting, the movement is forward and linear, the townspeople flee the streets and watch from windows or sidewalks. One man will continue moving forward after the fight. To Leone, whose movement is circular (and triangular, when the shoot-out is three-way) the survivor moves simply toward another such shoot-out.

The Opera Of Violence: If Leone were not Italian, the opera metaphor might seem extravagant, but if we consider opera's sense of heightened realism, which makes melodrama acceptable as reality, we can understand the similarity. In Leone's films, the effect is achieved by simplifying the storytelling to the individual characters' basic emotions, and then using his tools to heighten those emotions. Thus Leone reduces the Western to its essence, the battle of the killers with the guns, and then heightens the impact of that battle. The slow and involved build-up to the inevitable confrontation has always been a feature of Westerns, but to Leone the pacing is punctuated by other moments of fierce violence. And as the side issues of the plot fall (often literally) by the wayside, what we wind up with is the ritual confrontation of men

11

taking place within the confined parameters of the gunfighter's world. Besides opera, this also suggests bullfighting, and in this Leone had another precursor in Westerns: Budd Boetticher, as we shall see later.

We've already seen how other directors recognised the stylised and ritual nature of the gunfight. What Leone does is take those shots of the boots, of the eyes, and of the guns, and hold them. He builds the ritual to heighten the impact of the final instant. And he gives the players equal billing. Fuller shows us only Sullivan's eyes, leaving Ericson in full face as he panics (Ericson, by the way, smokes a cheroot remarkably similar to Eastwood's, but throws it away before drawing). Leone cuts from eyes to eyes, seeing not the differences in the characters but their similarity. With the characters thus levelled, the gunfight has become, not the pay-off of the movie but its raison d'être, not a means to an end (resolution of some other issue) but the end and resolution itself. It recognises that violence was the essence of the Western myth.

It was this attitude that opened the doors for a new sense of violence in the Western, but it's important to note the qualitative difference of Leone's depiction of violence. What he skews is the moral code of the gunfighter. Leone's gunfighter's are more callous, death is more sudden, for less reason, than Western conventions called for. There is a cynicism to it; people may be shot for no good reason at all, simply because they are around shooters. Gunmen may get what they want, and then kill someone anyway. But there is none of the American fascination with the process of dying, the art of killing. Death is not choreographed as it is in *Bonnie And Clyde* or *The Wild Bunch* (1969). Instead it comes as a sharp and final shock (think of the two riders shot out of their saddles by Harmonica early in *Once Upon A Time In The West*). Rarely is it contemplative (Frank gets enough time to realise why he is dying; Cheyenne complains that his own death is coming too slowly). Leone concentrates on the mentality of death, amplifying those sadistic gunfighters who stem from Jack Palance in *Shane* (1953). His West is populated with dozens of Henry Silvas (*Tall T* (1957)), John Ericsons (*Forty Guns*), Lee Marvins (*The Man Who Shot Liberty Valence* (1962)): psychopaths with no moral reason behind their acts, simply the indulgence of their one skill. All that may separate The Man With No Name from them is his greater skill.

This is not to say Leone's films lack graphic violence. Apart from *Once Upon A Time In The West*, all his films contain torture scenes which hark back to his apparent fascination with bizarre and perverse ways of inflicting pain, to a specific purpose. In *A Fistful Of Dollars* Joe is tortured, and he returns to town to save Silvanito from more. In *For A Few Dollars More* the gang have their way with the two "bounty-keelers" while Indio also tortures Tomaso with the sound of his wife and child being killed. *The Good, The Bad And The Ugly* features Wallace's torture of Tuco, while the prison-camp orchestra plays, and scenes cut from *Duck, You Sucker* showed Villega's torture in far more detail. *Once Upon A Time In America* begins with Fat Moe being tortured and hanged. But the real change in Leone's approach to violence is the motivation, and the moral lesson, behind it.

The Mood: Cynicism As Politics: Many read the violence in Leone's films as the very reason for their existence, and certainly for the existence of his heroes. Traditionally in Westerns, violence was presented as a means to an end, a noble end, and it was the audience's good luck that the hero usually was better at it than the villain. In Leone's West, violence is an end in and of itself. In the real world, the 'good guys' are not always the most adept at violence, and all Leone's audience can hope for is that the men who are best at it are something better than evil.

"Ford is an optimist, I am a pessimist," Leone told Massimo Moscati in 1978. "When Ford's characters open a window, what they see in the end is a horizon full of hope, while mine are always afraid of getting a bullet through the eyes…so for me Ford's best movie was one of his last, *The Man Who Shot Liberty Valence*, where he rediscovered pessimism." Leone would go on to compare Ford's optimism with Frank Capra's, both were successfully assimilated newcomers to America. At the same time, he was fond of citing Ford as one of the many 'Europeans' (Ford was born in Portland, Maine, to Irish immigrant parents), like Zinnemann or Lang, who made great Westerns.

Leone's characters are not so much pessimistic as cynical, having faith only in their own strength, and recognising that authority comes from strength rather than moral superiority. Leone's cynicism came from many roots, beyond what some might see as typical 'realism' in the land of Machiavelli and the Borgias. He saw what his father's political beliefs cost him in career terms, and he saw how little change those ideals made in the real political world. His childhood dreams of American supermen were shattered when he actually encountered GIs during the fall of Italy. And his heroes of the American cinema turned out to sport serious feet of clay when he began working with them in the Italian film industry.

For whatever reason, the mood of his films chimed in perfectly with the irreverence of the 1960s generation, deflating those who claimed to set society's tone. In Leone's films these are corrupt sheriffs, absurd generals or greedy businessmen. These figures are standard Western characters. The difference in Leone's films is that no hero fights against them to prove them wrong, or to prove them aberrations within society. Leone's heroes manage to do the best for themselves, to keep cool, as the phrase went, but (sometimes) care. However, to keep such characters alive in a world where most of the might is allied to the power of the status quo, Leone needed a very special sort of world.

Realism And Fantasy: Leone's training grounded him in a wide spectrum of Italian film, starting with the neo-realists, moving on to the popular Italian genre films, and then to the visiting American productions at Cinecittà. Although many commentators see the rejection of neo-realism as a key to Leone's work (he never made a film set in the present, indeed, the closest he gets is 1968 in *Once Upon A Time In America,* released in 1984) it might be fairer to see his work as embracing an early form of what came to be called magic realism (one of Leone's unconsummated projects was a TV mini-series of Gabriel Garcia Marquez's *One Hundred Years Of Solitude*). This is most evident in *Once Upon A Time In America,* but all his movies, even those like *The Good, The Bad And The Ugly* or *Duck, You Sucker,* rooted in specific historical times, have a timeless quality. Clocks and watches will recur as motifs throughout his work, often keying flashbacks that are always a part of the action of the present, not just events happening in the past.

Leone also used his passion for both historical and artistic detail to create the impression of reality. He was a keen scholar of Western history, who did much period research in weapons, architecture, costuming and furnishing. He was heavily influenced by the art direction of Alexander Trauner, and was lucky enough to rely on Carlo Simi, who would be art director on all his films after *Colossus Of Rhodes,* except *Duck, You Sucker.* Although not every detail is historically accurate (for example the Navy Colts in *The Good, The Bad And The Ugly* have been modified, anachronistically, from cap and ball to cartridges) the overall impression is one of verisimilitude. In addition to period detail, Leone always showed the West as an area of dirt, dust and filth. Meals are simple, manners atrocious, and the overall effect is to convince the audience that we really are in a land beyond the reaches of society. Thus the fantasy of superhuman gunmen performing their heroic shooting feats, in this context of heightened reality, creates a product which convinces us at the same time as it charms us. It is exactly the same process by which fairy tales win us over when we are children. It is the same sense of being 'better' than real that makes the narration of Raymond Chandler or the dialogues (monologues?) of George V Higgins convincing, even though we know humans don't really talk that way.

Soundtrack: The Sounds Of Silence: The Leone soundtrack was more than just the score composed by Ennio Morricone, though Morricone's use of individual instruments, including human voice, to provide the equivalent of sound effects is crucial. Morricone orchestrates to evoke emotions (is there any theme more powerful, in the traditional sense, than Jill's as it rises over the wide shots at the end of *Once Upon A Time In The West?*) but, as Frayling puts it, Leone also uses music for punctuation, as a way of commenting on the action, of adding comic relief, of giving the ruthless gunplay a more human glow. Thus the little trills which accompany the return of Eastwood's gun to its holster lighten the callous method in which he eliminates adversaries.

Just as Leone's West is focused on individuals, Morricone's use of the lone human voice, or of the chanting grunts of a small choir, or the isolated solo instrument, brings the epic scale of Western soundtracks back to a more individual level. It is constantly redirecting your attention back to the characters, and away from the general sweep of the West.

As important as the music is the use of natural sound. The opening of *Once Upon A Time In The West* is orchestrated to the sound of a squeaking windmill and a dripping water tank. The massacre that follows is preceded by a chorus of clicking cicadas. These sounds fill the screen like music, but with the effect of heightening the reality of the upcoming scene, even as it drifts further and further into violent melodrama.

Morricone delighted in amplifying the rituals of gunfights. In *For A Few Dollars More* he is at his most audacious. Having already established a link between Indio's watch music and a church organ, he then adds, for the ultimate shoot-out, in quick succession, trumpet, guitar and carillon, giving the *deguello*, already a standard of Westerns, a whole new life.

The overall effect was to create a new sort of Western movie, one whose impact on audiences, and on the genre would be immediate and profound. But to understand just how profound, we need to recall just where the Western was when Leone came onto the scene, as unheralded as The Man With No Name on his donkey in *A Fistful Of Dollars*.

Once Upon A Time In Western Movies

Imagine you're in a movie house in 1967, anticipating your first glimpse of what they're already calling Spaghetti Westerns, made in Italy. Maybe as a youngster you saw and enjoyed, in a light-hearted way, those Steve Reeves Hercules movies, with the dubbing that makes every line seem amusing, no matter how seriously intended. Maybe you've just heard some of the word-of-mouth beginning to build around *A Fistful Of Dollars*. Maybe you're a Western fan, and will see any of the films *Variety* calls 'oaters.' Or maybe you've just wandered in, expecting nothing.

The opening titles are animated, the soundtrack a combination of gunshots and strange music, echoing traditional Western themes but also possessing an eerie spiritual quality. Then, as if out of the sun, a figure draped in a Mexican *serape* rides a mule across a bleak, dusty landscape. It's no Mexican, it's Clint Eastwood, whom you've seen as Rowdy Yates on TV's *Rawhide,* only he's no longer clean-cut, but dirty, bearded, and smoking a foul, cut-off cheroot. He stops for water and encounters a child in distress, a woman held prisoner. He watches, and rides on. He enters the town, passing a hanged man on a horse. He is greeted by a group of eccentrics worthy of a Beckett play, then he is harassed by a gang of gunmen who, in best Western tradition, use violence for recreation. After getting the lay of the land, he stages a showdown with his four tormentors, telling them to apologise to his mule, who is sensitive. They take this request in the spirit in which it is delivered, and he kills them all, reprising Toshiro Mifune (in *Yojimbo* (1961)) as he walks away by correcting the order he placed in advance with the coffin-maker.

You pinch yourself, perhaps, and wonder 'what am I seeing? THIS is what they call a Western?' And you realise, it sure enough is.

John Ford, at a point in his career when he was arguably the best-known director in Hollywood, famously stood up at a Directors' Guild meeting called by Cecil B DeMille to blacklist and hound suspected Commies, and speaking against DeMille and his 'loyalty oaths' introduced himself by saying, "My name is John Ford. I make Westerns." I believe Ford intended more from his statement than the unnecessary self-deprecation usually read into it. Perhaps instinctively, he was putting himself into a particularly double-edged American context. First, in terms of values, Ford was recalling the myths which Western movies had helped propagate, those essentially American values which defined the country's self-image, and even more important for our discussion of Sergio Leone, defined America for generations of movie-goers abroad. He was putting himself forward as a representative of those values, and lending the weight of that to his own thoughts that the blacklisters were operating in opposition to them.

Second, and maybe more importantly, Ford was calling on the specifically Hollywood context of what 'making Westerns' meant. It was a genre which had often been the financial backbone of the industry, but had rarely provided the respectability sought by members of 'the Academy.' Ford's only Oscar for Best Picture was for *How Green Was My Valley* (1941); he had previously won Best Director Oscars for *The Informer* (1935) and *The Grapes Of Wrath* (1940) and would win another for *The Quiet Man* (1952). None of these films was a Western. In fact, until 1990, Wesley Ruggles' *Cimarron* (1931) was the only Western to win a Best Picture Oscar, but *Cimarron* was based on an epic novel by Edna Ferber, which was 'bigger' than a Western. So when John Ford wanted to make a brief speech defining 'Americanism' as he saw it, he specifically defined himself using the kind of films which DeMille and his ilk might have seen as beneath their considerable dignity. It was Ford's way of puncturing pomposity and getting down to business.

Yet, it's easy to argue that as Ford spoke, the Hollywood Western was reaching its apex. It was a time when big-budget A-features were being produced across the board - classic mainstream popular films like *Red River* (1948), *High Noon* and *Shane*. In the wake of those hits, the 1950s became a golden age for Western B-movies, with directors like Anthony Mann and Budd Boetticher producing series of small masterpieces.

The 1950s boom also extended to television. By 1958 Westerns made up more than a quarter of all prime-time TV shows in America, and 9 of the top 11 programmes in the ratings. They also comprised a large chunk of the syndicated shows which made up the crucial Saturday morning viewing for most of the nation's youngsters. In that same year Hollywood produced 54 Western features.

The TV wave crested in the early 1960s, at which point many of the more talented people in television were making their way into features. But the number of feature films declined rapidly as well, and those that were produced might best be defined in terms of three Es: elegy, epic and era.

In the early 60s, Ford made his myth-shattering *The Man Who Shot Liberty Valence,* the cynical *Two Rode Together* (1961), the revisionist *Sergeant Rutledge* (1960), and the bitter elegy *Cheyenne Autumn* (1964). Howard Hawks rode off into the sunset with *El Dorado* (1967). Even young film-makers, like Sam Peckinpah, who graduated from television Westerns, ploughed the same furrow: Peckinpah's second feature *Ride The High Country* (1962)(aka *Guns In The Afternoon,* perhaps a better title) is arguably the finest elegy to the Western hero ever filmed. At the same time, Hollywood was trying to 'super-size' films to combat the growing encroachment of TV. They produced overblown epics in all genres, but the most typical Western was *How The West Was Won* (1962). In fact, a simple way to accomplish the feat of time travel suggested in the opening paragraphs would be to watch *How The West Was Won* and then, immediately afterwards, view *A Fistful Of Dollars,* and see it through new eyes.

Finally, there was a run of anachronistic Westerns, films like *Lonely Are The Brave* (1962), *Hud* (1963) or *The Misfits* (1961), using recognisable Western characters set in modern times as if the Western era had been exhausted. In *Lonely Are The Brave,* for example, Kirk Douglas' cowboy eludes modern lawmen, only to be run over by an interstate trucker, in a collision foreshadowed throughout the film.

The Western had been proclaimed dead before, probably first when sound came into vogue and Westerns were relegated to poverty row. But by the time *A Fistful Of Dollars* first appeared (made in 1964, it would not be released in the USA until 1967), the Western movie really was in trouble. As Geoffrey O'Brien puts it, 'this sustained plundering of the genre's resources had by 1960 pretty much run it dry. The generation that grew up in the 1950s knew the mechanics and conventions so well that new forms of excess and rule-breaking were required to maintain excitement.' That generation would come of age just as Leone's films burst onto the scene of this cinematic depression to indulge in excess and break rules like the Rojos themselves.

This brief study will show that Leone did not come to this *sui generis,* but rather from a keen appreciation of America, America's cinematic West, and of cinema itself. His genius was that he was able to isolate elements from the mythology of the West, and use a sensibility refined by European traditions, especially Italian cinema and perhaps opera, to amplify them. He appears to have thought in cinematic terms from the start—seeing stories in visual terms. The story of his working relationship with Clint Eastwood has been retold many times: Leone's limited English included the phrase "Watch me, Clint" and he would literally act out scenes as he visualised them in his mind. Eli Wallach noted that despite the seeming continual chaos on a Leone set, the director always had a clear idea of what he was aiming for, and was quick to see how improvisation and suggestion could be incorporated into those ideas. This was something he learned in the cauldron of the Italian film industry in the 1950s, both assisting Americans and working on Italian films which were often scripted by battalions, with ideas being exchanged frequently. Leone fitted right in, for it was a world into which he had born.

The Directors' Apprentice

Sergio Leone's whole life was lived in cinema. He was born January 3rd, 1929 in Rome, the only child of Vincenzo Leone and Edvige Valcarenghi. Leone's parents met in the film industry. His father came from Naples, had attended law school there, and then began working in films under the pseudonym Roberto Roberti (because his parents did not approve of his working in such a disreputable business). His mother, an actress whose stage name was Bice Walerian, came from Rome, where her family had run a hotel near the Spanish Stairs. After marrying, she gave up the screen, but it would be another 13 years before Sergio was born, by which time his father was nearly 50.

Leone's parents made the first successful Italian Western, *La Vampira Indiana (The Indian Vamp)* in 1913, with Roberti directing and Walerian playing the Indian Princess of the title. She leads a life of crime on behalf of her brother, before being faced down by the daughter of an innocent man who had been condemned to die for her crimes. As Christopher Frayling, Leone's biographer, points out in the documentary *Viva Leone,* this was also the time that Puccini's opera *The Girl Of The Golden West* was playing in New York, and that could well be considered the first Spaghetti Western.

Roberti also directed one of the early Maciste films. Maciste, as played by Bartolomeo Pagano (whom Leone would claim was discovered by his father) was the original hero of peplum (sword and sandal) films, named after the short kilts worn by the Greek heroes.

Roberto Roberti became one of the top directors of the Italian silent cinema, perhaps best known for a series of light genre comedies made with the Neapolitan diva Francesca Bertoni. Despite his stature, with the coming of the sound era, Vincenzo Leone went without work for a full decade, 1929-39. Perhaps it was because of his growing devotion to the Left. Or perhaps it was because of a personal grudge - Leone wrote a screenplay in 1923 based on the story *Claudia Particella* written a decade earlier by a young journalist named Benito Mussolini. Or it may have just been bad luck. Perhaps authorities mistook Leone for a Jewish surname (later in World War Two, Leone's father tried to help Jews avoid deportation to Germany). At any rate, the family did not suffer, as Leone had both savings from his better days and a fine collection of antiques which could be sold off. Sergio would inherit his father's love of antiques and furnishings, something that can be seen in the lavish detail paid to sets in all his films.

As a youngster, Sergio was equally entranced by the puppet theatre of the south of Italy, Neapolitan glove puppets (his father, of course, could speak in the dialect of Naples), Sicilian rod puppets, American comic strips, pulp fiction, and cinema. Charlie Chaplin would be the film-maker most cited by Leone as a formative influence - he was fond of quoting Chaplin when he said that America was "a nation of children." In the late 70s Dino De Laurentiis offered Leone the chance to direct the movie which eventually became Mike Hodges' high-camp entertainment *Flash Gordon* (1980), but Leone turned him down because he wanted to remain faithful to Alex Raymond's original Sunday comic pages.

Leone's childhood was spent in Trastevere, in the suburbs of Rome. Certainly one senses in *Once Upon A Time In America* the memory of Leone's own street-urchin days being filtered through to his vision of Jewish street urchins in New York's Lower East Side. Much of the spirit of one of his cherished projects, a movie about his childhood which would have been called *Viale Glorioso* lives on in the sheer exuberance of childhood energy in those scenes. And images of Chaplin as well, in the scene where Patsy eats the charlotte russe he has bought to exchange for Peggy's favours.

When Roberti resumed his directing career, young Sergio spent much of his time on film sets. He made his on-screen debut in 1945, as an extra in *The Madman Of Marchechiano*, directed by his father. His parents didn't want him to follow them into the film business, and he began studying for the law, as his father wished. But just as his father had, he would go against his parents' wishes and abandon the law for movies. He developed an insatiable appetite for both films and the camaraderie of film-makers. He watched the American movies which flooded the post-war Italian market, and which were responsible, in a business sense, for creating the conditions which drew American film-makers to Italy in the 1950s. But at the same time he also found himself, through his father's contacts, a bit player at the centre of a fascinating era of Italian cinema.

He worked as an unpaid assistant on Vittorio DeSica's *The Bicycle Thieves* (1948), and appears as an extra in one scene. He also worked as an unpaid assistant to Carmine Gallone, a friend of his father's who made a series of filmed operas, and on *Fabiola (Fighting Gladiator,*

1947) directed by Alessandro Biasetti, as the Italian film industry began to discover the historical genre films which would later result in the peplum industry.

When Leone's family left Rome in 1949 (his father would never direct again), Sergio stayed in the city, getting a job as a paid assistant on a film directed by his godfather, Mario Camerini, *Musolino The Brigand* (1950). Camerini was one of the leading directors of the Italian comedies of manners known as telefoni bianchi (white telephones). Leone moved into the house of the director Mario Bonnard, another of his father's friends, where he would continue to live until he got married in 1960. His filmography for the next few years covers a wide spectrum of the contemporary Italian cinema. For Bonnard, who could claim to have made the very first neo-realist film, *Campo Di Fiori* (1943), he assisted on some seven films, taking an increasingly large role as Bonnard grew older and less energetic. He also worked with the comic actor/director Aldo Fabrizi completing *They've Stolen A Tram* (1954) which Bonnard had begun. It would not be the first time Leone would be among those finishing a Bonnard project. The original story for *They've Stolen A Tram* came from Luciano Vincenzoni, who would have a fruitful and also contentious relationship as one of Leone's main writers.

Leone also worked for the producers Dino De Laurentiis and Carlo Ponti on a number of films directed by Luigi Comencini and Mario Soldati. On Comencini's *La Trata Della Bianca* (1952), where Leone was credited as 'production secretary', the film editor was Nino Baragli, who would become a key part of Leone's stock company; both Bonnard and Soldati employed a director of photography named Tonino Delli Colli, who would go on to lens Leone's finest films.

Leone was receiving a firm grounding in the mechanics of the movie industry. One gets the sense of the atmosphere at Cinecittà in Rome as something like a huge melting pot, with the inevitable cross-fertilisation of ideas. Frayling makes the point that the directors who received artistic acclaim outside Italy (Rossellini, Fellini, Pasolini, Antonioni) were all northern Italians, while the bulk of Italian cinema was being produced by those from Rome and the south, in the studio-like atmosphere of Cinecittà. It is a point echoed by Luc Moullet, who makes the divide between the 'auteur cinema' and the cinema 'based on the conventions of genre.' This north/south divide would echo throughout Leone's career. But there was also considerable cross-pollination. Fellini would pay homage to Cinecittà and DeSica would move from *The Bicycle Thieves* to genre films with ease. While Leone saw both sides first-hand, he was also deeply involved in the fabulous fantasy quality of American films. This combination gave him a cinematic background far more like that of the early Hollywood directors he so admired than most of his European or American contemporaries.

In this collective atmosphere of film-making in Rome, Leone began contributing to scripts, and script-doctoring. Much of the scripting process appears to have been done by committee (in the sense of conversations in a café or a bar, as well as the more literal sense of the many names listed on Italian films, which generally credit more of those involved at each stage of the process than American films do). Soon he was receiving script credits, the first of which was on *Nel Segno Di Roma* (1958), directed by Guido Brignone, another of his father's generation. When Brignone fell ill the film was completed by Michelangelo Antonioni, who apparently followed Brignone's instructions to the letter, letting none of his own style seep into a film (belying that north/south, auteur/hack divide).

Nel Segno Di Roma (literally, under the sign, or standard, of Rome) starred Georges Marchal, who would go on to star in *Colossus Of Rhodes,* as the Roman Consul in Spain, and Anita Ekberg (before Fellini made her a star) as the Queen of Palmyra who winds up tamed by her Roman lord. Nino Baragli was again the film editor. This was one of the first peplum films picked up and distributed in the USA (retitled S*ign Of The Gladiator*, although no gladiators appear in the film). Its success at the American box office sparked the craze for sword and sandal epics which kept Cinecittà busy before the rise of Spaghetti Westerns.

This boom led to the commissioning of another major project, where Leone, like Antonioni, would take over from another director. The director was his surrogate father, Mario Bonnard. The film was *The Last Days Of Pompeii* (1959), a sword and sandal epic to be filmed in Spain starring Hercules himself, Steve Reeves, and the wonderful German actress Christina Kaufman, whom Leone would claim to have discovered

Bonnard's health was frail, and soon after arriving in Spain he preferred to return to Rome and direct another film. So Leone, who had been scheduled to handle the second unit, took over the direction. He assembled a team which reads like a Spaghetti Western roster. Sergio Corbucci took over the second unit, with Enzo Barboni (who, as EB Clucher, would direct the Trinity Westerns) as his cameraman. Franco Giraldi, uncredited, would film interior sequences. Corbucci and assistant director Duccio Tessari collaborated on the script, as did Leone. These men would wind up directing more than thirty Italian Westerns and, according to Corbucci, the inspiration for their trademark Spanish locations came while they filmed *The Last Days Of Pompeii*.

The Italian muscle epics tended to be more action-packed than their larger scale American counterparts; the US films (*Quo Vadis* (1951) and *Ben Hur* (1959), for example) being more interested in historical issues of the Roman Empire and Christianity. With *The Last Days Of Pompeii*, as he would do with his Westerns, Leone established a sort of middle ground, widening the scope of the Italian approach into a more epic American approach or, if you prefer, livening up the epic style with more action.

Again reflecting that Italian cultural divide, many of Leone's collaborators from the north refer to him in terms that suggest he was a relatively 'uncivilised' man, without artistic pretensions. Virtually all his colleagues refer to an almost legendary cheapness, something which may have been honed by working as an assistant director (and certainly wouldn't have hurt his working at that job).

But without exception, they also describe a director who, on set, knew exactly what he wanted visually and was relatively open to collaborative ideas. He worked quickly and efficiently, and learnt how to make the most from what was often fairly standard material. It was in sharp contrast to his experiences working on the second units of lavish American productions.

The Hell With Dialog,
Let's Kill Something*

*Slogan on T-shirts worn by James Best's 2nd unit in *The Stunt Man*

There is a theory that the emphasis on action in the Italian peplum movies, and in the Westerns which would follow them, came about because the film-makers at Cinecittà were kept busy through the 1950s and early 1960s working on the second units of the American epics then being filmed in Italy, and thus they developed a feeling and flair for action. This ignores their work in the Italian cinema, but it is fair to say that the experience of working with the US productions was a key factor for many of the Italians, including Leone.

Throughout his apprenticeship in Italian cinema, Leone also worked on American productions, usually as an assistant director to the second units. Americans were filming epics in Italy partly because costs were lower and partly because the Italians already has a certain amount of expertise in the staging of such genre films. Also, the Americans were required by law to spend some of their profits from the Italian box office in Italy, so filming there was a way of spending that money.

In 1950 Leone worked on the very first of the American costume epics to be filmed at Cinecittà, Mervyn LeRoy's *Quo Vadis* (1951). The difference between American and Italian budgets soon became apparent, as did the difference between the Americans' more hierarchical chain of command and the more communal Italian approach. Leone, only 21, was in charge of marshalling extras.

He became more involved in the making of *Helen Of Troy* (1955) directed by Robert Wise. It's possible to see elements in the Helen story resurfacing in *A Fistful Of Dollars*, where Ramon Rojo's desire for Marisol is the cause of his coming into direct conflict with the Man With No Name. Is this the face which launched a thousand bullets?

The stunt director was Yakima Canutt, Hollywood's finest Western stuntman, the man who had doubled for John Wayne in *Stagecoach* (1939). Working with Canutt as a stuntman was Benito Steffanelli, who went on to be Leone's stunt director and play small roles in many of his films. Wise's production soon fell behind schedule when its Trojan horse burned to the ground. Raoul Walsh flew in from America to help

Wise as an uncredited second unit director. Leone wanted nothing more than to talk Westerns with Walsh, but the veteran director told him simply "the Western is finished."

Leone worked with Fred Zinnemann, who had directed *High Noon*, on *A Nun's Story* (1958). Location filming was in the Congo, which was then in the throes of a revolution against the Belgians. Leone later paid homage to *High Noon* in his films. Zinnemann's art director was the legendary Alexander Trauner, whose attention to detail impressed Leone; he would rely on his own designer, Carlo Simi's brilliance for the look of his pictures and was himself obsessed with details of costume and set decoration, even those which couldn't be seen in a shot.

Finally, Leone worked on the greatest of all the American epics made at Cinecittà, William Wyler's *Ben Hur* (1959), which again allowed Leone the experience of working with Yakima Canutt, one of three credited second unit directors. Canutt had staged the chariot race for Fred Niblo's silent *Ben Hur* (1926), and now would attempt to outdo himself 33 years later, while Andrew Marton handled second unit direction.

Leone spent more than a decade in a full and varied apprenticeship. A number of sources make the point that Leone was still regarded very much as a youngster by the older generation of directors who had been colleagues of his father's, and certainly this did not seem to bother him on the surface, because he appears to have been in no burning hurry to ascend the ladder to directing his own films. One can sense a certain amount of reticence, and again, many of his collaborators agree that he was extremely insecure once placed in the position of making his own films. And although he had an unusually sure idea of what it was he wanted on film, he was always besieged by doubts about whether he would be able to get it done successfully or, once done, if he would ever be able to do it again.

But, as Frayling notes, *The Last Days of Pompeii* was the first time Leone was working on a film surrounded by his contemporaries, rather than those of his father or legends from America. That must have done something for his confidence, or perhaps he just enjoyed the experience of being in charge more than he had anticipated. At the same time, in 1960, Leone got married, and finally moved out of Mario Bonnard's house. *The Last Days Of Pompeii* was a huge box-office success, in Italy and worldwide. Though Leone didn't share in the financial rewards, its success brought him another muscle epic to direct.

Colossus Of Rhodes (1960)

Italy/Spain/France

USA Distributor: MGM

Running Times: Italy 142 mins, USA 128 mins, UK 127 mins

Cast: Rory Calhoun (Dario), Lea Massari (Diala), Georges Marchal (Peliocles), Conrado Sammartin (Thar), Angel Aranda (Koros), Mabel Karr (Mirte), Mimmo Palmara (Chares), Roberto Camardiel (Serse) Alfio Caltabianco/Alf Randall (Creonte), Jorge Rigaud (Lisippo), Yann Larvor (Mahor), Carlo Tamberlane (Semone), Felix Fernandez (Carete), Antonio Casas (Ambassador), Fernando Calzado (Sidione)

Crew: Director: Sergio Leone, Story and Screenplay: Ennio DeConcini, Sergio Leone, Cesare Seccia, Luciano Martino, Aggio Savioli, Luciano Chitarrini, Carlo Gualtieri, Director of Photography: Antonio Lopez Ballesteros, Second Unit Photography: Emilio Foriscot, Music: Angelo Lavagnino, Film Editor: Eraldo DaRoma, Art Director: Ramiro Gomez, Costumes: Vittorio Rossi, Choreography: Carla Ranalli, Executive Producer: Michele Scaglione, Sculptor of the Colossus: Socrate Valzanis

Story: Rhodes, 280BC. Greek war hero Dario, whose mother hailed from Rhodes, is visiting for some much needed vacation. At the dedication of the Colossus, which stands astride the entrance to Rhodes' harbour, Dario witnesses an assassination attempt on King Serse. The assassin's sister Mirte and four other brothers are leaders of a rebel faction, and resolve to approach Dario to seek Greek help in overthrowing the tyrant. Dario, however, is busy pursuing Diala, daughter of Carete, who designed the Colossus. She lures him into a labyrinth beneath the palace; Dario emerges into a meeting where Serse and his advisor Thar secretly plot an alliance with Phoenicia. Unknown to the plotters, Dario has paid no attention.

The rebel brothers attempt to kidnap Dario, but are chased away by his uncle. Dario decides to return to Greece. However, Serse has banned all exit from Rhodes, afraid Dario will warn the Greeks. Mirte gets Dario on her brothers' ship, but when they attempt to leave the ship is destroyed by molten lead poured from the Colossus. The brothers are captured, and tortured, and a letter intended for Dario to carry to Greece convinces Thar he is a spy.

Meanwhile, searching for his brothers, the youngest, Mahor discovers that the boatloads of Phoenician slaves arriving in Rhodes are actually soldiers, brought by Thar who plans to kill Serse and rule Rhodes as a Phoenician protectorate. Mahor and the rebels rescue his brothers and Dario before they can be sacrificed to Baal, and after Dario has refused Diala's offer of freedom if he will rat out the rebels.

Fleeing to caves in the Stone Desert, the rebels draw straws for a six-man suicide mission to set free 1,000 rebel soldiers imprisoned underneath the Colossus. Dario sneaks away and asks Diala's help in getting him inside the Colossus, and tells her to warn the rebels in the caves should he not succeed. He is followed to this rendezvous by Mirte.

Inside the Colossus, it turns out Diala is in league with Thar. Dario is captured and Carete, who has just invented the catapult, learns of his daughter's betrayal and is killed. After a fight on the arms of the Colossus, Dario escapes and returns to the caves to find rebels massacred. Mirte and Mahor are convinced Dario has betrayed them, but he manages to escape and rescue the brothers from execution in the circus. As Dario tries to alert Serse to the Phoenician plot, Thar's forces kill the King, and battle erupts.

Thar signals the Phoenicians to attack. As Dario enters the Colossus and frees the rebel prisoners he is captured, but Diala saves his life, ostensibly for later torture. Thar uses Carete's catapults against the rebels. However, just as the Phoenician fleet appears on the horizon, an earthquake topples the Colossus and destroys Rhodes. Diala is killed in the collapsing Colossus and Thar is killed by the brothers. Dario and Mirte escape, and ride off with the survivors to begin rebuilding Rhodes.

Background: There isn't much to identify *Colossus Of Rhodes* as a Leone film, in the context of his work to come as a director, nor to separate it from the run of peplum movies, apart from an inventiveness and intensity in the rather homoerotic sadomasochistic torture scenes. Rory Calhoun is very much the outsider ("I'm a stranger here myself" he says at one point), and is identified as such by his simple costume, complete with white wrestling (or go-go) boots, and an arm-cocked pose holding his tunic. The pose and dress will change when he commits to the rebel Rhodesians' (sic) cause. It's hard not to see Calhoun's identity as an American actor dropped into a European genre film reflected in Dario. It's also easy to see the roots of the Eastwood character stemming from this very sense of dislocation.

But Calhoun's character actually owes more to Hitchcock, to whom is paid the movie's most obvious homage, with the Colossus serving as the same sort of set for fights that Mount Rushmore and the Statue of Liberty did for Hitchcock in *North By Northwest* (1959) and *Saboteur* (1942) respectively. Leone would later say he was specifically thinking of *North By Northwest* in trying to create a lighter-hearted, tongue-in-cheek peplum, with Calhoun (indeed, a sort of very poor man's Cary Grant) as the vacationer caught up in things beyond his ken. In fact, Calhoun plays the part so well we start to wonder how desperate the Greeks were for war heroes at the time!

The allusion to the Statue of Liberty is another intentional piece of irony, as Leone was careful to have the Colossus used as a prison for the freedom fighters, which gives its destruction by the Gods (via earthquake) a certain sort of inevitability. Leone told people he had intended to fashion the Colossus in the image of Mussolini, complete with hands on hips, but that didn't happen. However some of the Spanish producers were unaware that Leone's Colossus was indeed the statue, and assumed that it/he would be a Steve Reeves-type warrior!

There is an almost fetishistic attachment to ears in this film. In the film's best scene, Dario battles two of the rebel brothers while his uncle sleeps blissfully through the chaos, hearing nothing because he is wearing earplugs to mute out the sound of Rhodes' storms. Later, Peliocles is tortured by having a bell put over his head and rung, to shatter his eardrums. Finally, the Colossus' ear proves an exit for Dario, and as he battles soldiers on the statue's arm, more pour out through the ear.

A Fistful Of Motifs: We can see the foreshadowing of the Westerns to come when Dario and the rebels ride to the caves. The shots of the galloping horsemen are pure Western, and when they arrive there is a corral that could be out of a Mexican village. The scene where Dario sneaks back to Rhodes, followed by Mirte, is echoed in the two Dollars films. Leone loves to have his characters literally move the plot while others sleep (and dream). It's also hard not to see the influence of *The Magnificent Seven* in youngest brother Mathos' (strangely called Theo in his first scene) skill with throwing knives: he wears a beltful of them outside his tunic, echoing James Coburn, who was Leone's second choice (after Henry Fonda) to star in *A Fistful Of Dollars*.

There are three sides to the Rhodesian conflict: the tyrant King, his treacherous advisor in league with the Phoenicians, and the rebels. Dario, in effect, sits in between the three, not playing them off each other but bouncing between them like a handball between three walls.

Dario's riding off into the sunset with Mirte is a vivid contrast to *Once Upon A Time In The West,* where Harmonica rides off into the sunset with Cheyenne's corpse, after refusing the unstated offer to remain behind with Jill and build the new town of Sweetwater. Interestingly, Dario's uncle accompanies Dario and Mirte, on a mule. It's played for laughs, but the resonance of a mule was the sort of touch that might stick in Leone's playful mind when he sent The Man With No Name into San Miguel.

Another resonating gimmick is the torture of one of the brothers over a lion pit in the circus. He is hung by ropes to each arm, and an archer cuts the ropes with arrows, an image which returns in Blondie and Tuco's business arrangement, and the unfortunate death of Blondie's Shorty. Also in the circus, the brothers are tortured by a chariot with blades protruding from its wheels, an echo of the chariot race in *Ben Hur*.

Colossal Trivia: The starring role in the film was originally given to John Derek, the dashing former Tarzan actor who at that point was married to Ursula Andress, and who would proceed to trade her in for newer models, namely Linda Evans and Bo Derek over the years. Derek had played in *The Ten Commandments* (1956), which was a selling point in peplum terms. Leone had problems with Derek from the start, fuelled partly by insecurity as Derek appeared to be usurping the director's prerogatives on set. Derek was fired, and Calhoun, who happened to be in Rome, replaced him the next day.

The Carla Ranalli who choreographed the dance sequences in the debauched banquet at King Serse's was Mrs. Sergio Leone, whom he had married just before filming began. Ranalli was a ballet dancer at the Rome Opera;.they remained married until Leone's death. Leone would later claim that the only reason he agreed to direct *Colossus Of Rhodes* was to get enough money for their honeymoon.

Verdict: Colossus Of Rhodes has its moments of humour, though it's not quite the peplum equivalent of the Trinity films. There are a few striking scenes. It also has some turgid dialogue and Calhoun sometimes seems woefully out of place. 2/5

No More Swords Or Sandals

Strangely, for a man whose reputation is based on genre films, Leone, having completed his first feature as a director, did not grab the next chance to jump back into the director's saddle. He appears to have had no desire to continue directing sword and sandal movies. Instead, he worked on the script of *The Seven Challenges* (1960, directed by Primo Zeglio) whose story involved the Great Khan ordering feuding chieftains to settle their differences in a series of one-on-one duels. He also wrote the original treatment and worked on the screenplay of *Romulus And Remus* (1961) directed by Sergio Corbucci, who went on to direct a number of key Spaghetti Westerns. Like *The Last Days Of Pompeii, Romulus And Remus* could be considered a great melting pot for the birth of the Spaghetti Western, reuniting many of the same talents. Corbucci, *Colossus Of Rhodes* writer Luciano Martino and Duccio Tessari (who would help script *A Fistful Of Dollars*) all contributed to the screenplay. Enzo Barboni was director of photography. Franco Giraldi was the second unit director. Benito Steffanelli was in charge of the stunts, and Carlo Simi was the designer. Leone contributed to one more screenplay - a 1962 costume drama, *Under The Flag Of Allah*, set in Moorish Spain.

In 1961 Leone did his final second unit job for an American production, on Robert Aldrich's *Sodom And Gomorrah* (1963). Leone was actually credited as 'co-director' of the Italian version, which allowed the production access to Italian government funding. His main task was to supervise large-scale second unit work in Morocco.

The production went way over budget, and Aldrich and Leone each blamed the other for the bulk of the overrun, but the effect of this collaboration on Leone must have been considerable. The two men did not get along personally, and Leone professed shock and dismay at Aldrich's working methods, particularly because, as he stated in various interviews, he admired Aldrich's films greatly. In various interviews he cites numerous Aldrich's films, but never his Westerns, yet their influence is obvious in Leone's work.

It's easy to see the roots of *For A Few Dollars More* in Aldrich's *Vera Cruz* (1954), with its competing mercenaries, confederate major Gary Cooper as the old man and the amoral conman Burt Lancaster as the boy. *Vera Cruz*, set in Mexico in the time of Maximilian and Juarez, also prefigures Peckinpah, but its tone of cynicism and its ritualized violence would both appeal to Leone. In the 1950s Aldrich was one of America's most cynical directors; his version of Mickey Spillane's *Kiss Me Deadly* (1955), despised by Spillane, examines the violent nature of the Mike Hammer hero as a *reductio ad absurdam*, in much the same way Leone would reduce the Western hero to being defined by his violent acts. Aldrich's Freudian Western *The Last Sunset* (1961) ends with a brilliantly stylised and amplified shoot-out between Rock Hudson and the ever-flamboyant (at least in his Western roles) Kirk Douglas. But it is Aldrich's visually direct storytelling, his use of extreme close-ups and jarring edits, which seems to have influenced Leone the most; only Samuel Fuller was a more dynamic visual storyteller.

By this time, the craze for sword and sandal movies was beginning to run its course. The Americans, scared off by the huge cost overruns on epics like *Sodom And Gomorrah* or, more famously, *Cleopatra* (1963), abandoned the Italian film industry just at the time the bottom fell out of the peplum. Needing a new outlet at Cinecittà, Italian film-makers looked for other work. There were a few Westerns being produced in Europe, e.g. the German adaptations of the Western novels of Karl May were made in Spain. So perhaps Leone, with his love of American Westerns, and having seen the Spanish landscape while filming *Last Days Of Pompeii*, made some sort of cognitive leap. Then Enzo Barboni recommended he see Akira Kurosawa's *Yojimbo,* and the leap appears to have been almost instantaneous. He was immediately calling his colleagues and telling them to see the film, and had already conceived of redoing it as a Western. The rest, as they say, was history.

A Fistful Of Dollars (1964)

Working Title: The Magnificent Stranger

Italy/Spain/Germany

Running Times: Italy 100 mins, USA France 96 mins, UK 95 mins

Cast: (Note: Where English pseudonyms were used in the credits, the real name is given first, followed after the slash by the alias): Clint Eastwood (The Stranger), Marianne Koch (Marisol), Gian Maria Volonté/Johnny Wels (Ramon Rojo), Wolfgang Lukschy (John Baxter), Sieghardt Rupp (Esteban Rojo), Josef Egger/Joe Edger (Piripero, The Undertaker), Antonio Prieto (Miguel Rojo), Jose 'Pepe' Calvo (Silvanito, The Cantina Owner), Margherita Lozano (Consuela Baxter), Mario Brega/Richard Stuyvesant (Chico), Daniel Martin (Julian), Benito Stefanelli/Benny Reeves (Rubio)

Crew: Director: Sergio Leone/Bob Robertson, Producers: Arrigo/Harry Columbo & Giorgio/George Papi, Screenplay (Uncredited): Duccio Tessari, Victor A Catena, G Schock, Sergio Leone, based on *Yojimbo* by Ryuzo Kikushima and Akira Kurosawa, adapted by Leone, Dialogue: Mark Lowell, Director Of Photography: Massimo Dallamano/Jack Dalmas, Assisted by Frederico Larraya, Music: Ennio Morricone/Don Savio & Leo Nichols, Editor: Roberto Cinquini/Bob Quintle, Art Director & Costumes: Carlo Simi/Charles Simons, Second Unit Director: Franco Giraldi/Frank Prestland, Stunts: Bill Tomkins & Benito Stefanelli, Titles: Luigi Lardani, Musicians: Alessandro Allesandroni (Director, guitar, whistle, and choral arrangements), I Cantori Moderni (Choir), Edda dell'Orso (Soprano), Michele Lacerenza (Trumpet)

Location: La Pedrizia di Colemnar Viego, Almería (Spain)

Story: A stranger on a mule rides into the town of San Miguel, having observed, while stopping for water, the strange sight of a mother (Marisol) separated from her husband and child in houses that face each other. Entering the town, the stranger learns from the bell-ringer, cantina owner, and coffin-maker that the town is split between two families, the Baxters and the Rojos. Determining there is a profit in being in the middle of the two groups, The Man With No Name (or "Joe" as the coffin-maker dubs him) learns the Rojos are stronger. To impress them, he guns down four Baxter gunmen who taunted him (and his mule) when he rode into town.

Hired by Esteban Rojo, he meets the more dynamic brother, Ramon, who while impressed with the Stranger's gunslinging ability, insists a rifle is the stronger weapon. At the Rojo house, Joe learns that Marisol is kept as a virtual captive, the mistress of Ramon.

Joe and Silvanito watch as Ramon and his men, disguised as American soldiers, massacre a Mexican troop bringing gold to purchase Gatling guns from the Americans. Ramon suggests a truce with the Baxters, but Joe moves two dead soldiers to the local cemetery, selling

34

Consuela Baxter the information that the soldiers will confirm the Rojos' massacre, and telling the Rojos that the two have agreed to tell the Baxters. The Baxters and Rojos shoot it out at the cemetery, where Ramon 'kills' both soldiers with his Winchester. While the families shoot it out, Joe searches for the stolen money, only to be surprised by Marisol, whom he knocks out. He takes her to the Baxters, but the Rojos kidnap a Baxter son and arrange an exchange.

During the exchange, Marisol's son again runs to her, but Silvanito and Joe stop the Rojos from killing the child and father. That night, Joe sneaks away and kills Marisol's jailers, setting her and her family free and giving them money. When he returns to the Rojos house, Ramon is waiting for him.

Joe is tortured, but manages to escape. In the search for Joe, the Rojos finally attack the Baxters, setting fire to their house and killing them one by one, including Consuela, as they escape the fire. Joe watches this as he is spirited from the town in a coffin. Hiding out in a cave he recovers his strength and the use of his gun hand, while welding and fashioning a piece of metal.

The Rojos discover Silvanito has been helping Joe, and torture him. Joe emerges from an explosion, taunting Ramon, who shoots him repeatedly in the heart with the Winchester. But Joe rises from each shot. Joe matches his gun against Ramon's rifle in a single-bullet shoot-out, killing Ramon. He finishes off the Rojos, frees Silvanito and leaves town with the money from the arms deal, which he says he intends to return to the Mexican authorities.

Fathers & Sons: Leone was credited on the film as Bob Robertson, a touching homage to his father Roberto Roberti. Some of the pseudonyms were literal. For example, Volonté means 'well' (as in drawing water from) in Italian, while stuntman Benito Steffanelli adopted Benny Reeves in tribute to Steve Reeves, whom he had doubled in Hercules movies. Ennio Morricone's double pseudonym may reflect a tip of the hat to conductor Bruno Nicolai, who would conduct his score in *For A Few Dollars More*.

A Fistful of Motifs: The most prominent of Leone's recurring motifs is religious symbolism, and it's easy to view *A Fistful Of Dollars* as a sort of Christian allegory. Eastwood rides into town on a mule, is greeted by the bell-ringer Juan de Dios (John of God). He assumes various crucifixion poses throughout the film, starting with his hanging from a signpost when his mule bolts. When he is tortured he leaves town in a coffin (symbolically killed). He rises from the tomb (a cave) and returns to rise from the dead again as Ramon repeatedly 'kills' him with rifle shots to the heart.

Joe sets free Marisol (Mary), her husband Jose (Joseph) and baby Jesus. The Rojos' party from which he slips away is shot to resemble Leonardo's *Last Supper*.

Background: Looking back to *Colossus Of Rhodes*, Marianne Koch (Marisol) resembles and is costumed much like Mabel Kerr (Mirte). We see the parallel rides as Joe outraces the Rojos and Baxters to and from the cemetery. Just as Rory Calhoun sneaks away from the sleeping rebels, so Clint sneaks away from the Rojos - in each case they will not get away as cleanly as they thought.

A Fistful of Dollars is based on *Yojimbo*, but it is far more than a remake. Leone had seen the film on the recommendation of cameraman Enzo Barboni, and immediately urged his colleagues to see it as well. He quickly saw its possibilities as a story which could be returned to its American roots.

Akira Kurosawa was heavily influenced by American Westerns and thrillers, and had drawn on elements of Dashiell Hammett's *Red Harvest* in plotting out *Yojimbo*. It's hard not to see an echo of Hammett's nameless Continental Op in Leone's Man With No Name. Beyond the anonymity, both characters owe loyalty only to an internalised code of ethics, and both are prepared to lie as long as their lying keeps them in touch with their code.

As Leone became more sensitive to criticism, he would cite a different source for the original story: Carlo Goldoni's play, *Harlequin, Servant Of Two Masters,* but that link had actually been dredged up after the fact, in order to counter a plagiarism lawsuit by Kurosawa. In the end, Kurosawa received royalties from *A Fistful Of Dollars*, but his lawsuit was responsible for the English language release of the film (and *For A Few Dollars More)* being delayed until 1967.

There are many differences between *Yojimbo* and *A Fistful Of Dollars,* not least the basic motivation of the main characters. Toshiro Mifune's samurai appears to play the two merchant factions against each other as much for his own amusement as anything else - perhaps the legacy of a samurai with no master *(*ronin*).* Eastwood's 'Joe' is motivated by profit, although he winds up giving away some profit to help Marisol and is supposedly going to return the bulk of the rest to the Mexican government as the film ends.

More important than the mechanics of the story are the thematic and stylistic influences: Eastwood's cheroot serves the same purpose as the straw which is always in Mifune's mouth; combat is a ritual, which is important to the samurai. The identification of gunfighters as American samurai is crucial to all of Leone's Westerns.

Leone's fascination with American film provided other, more subtle, influences. Leone's pacing, cutting and use of extreme close-ups may owe something to Aldrich, but it's also easy to see Sam Fuller in the use of jarring cuts and extreme close-ups. Leone, like many film-makers, cited *Shane* as being crucial for showing what bullets did when they hit people, as well as the restrained style of Jack Palance as the gunman. He also loved Edward Dymytryk's *Warlock* (1959), which crucially distances the gunfighter, not just from frightened townspeople, but from other humans in general. A more direct, though overlooked, influence may be Robert Parrish's *The Wonderful Country* (1959), where Robert Mitchum becomes involved in a town dominated by gun-runners. His entrance, with bearded stubble and wearing a serape, is made as dust blows down an almost surreal main street populated by the same characters we find in the streets of Leone's Mexican villages.

But the key point is not the influences themselves, but what Leone did with them. As Clint Eastwood pointed out, Leone was the first to break that unwritten rule that the shooter and the victim couldn't be seen in the same shot. But he went even further, showing the Rojos taking great glee as they massacre the Baxters coming out of their burning house. They shoot the unarmed, they shoot down Consuela Baxter as well, laughing all the while. These reaction shots, apparently including some saved from earlier takes by editor Roberto Cinquini, are extended in the Italian version far longer than in the English cut.

Morricone's Music: A Fistful Of Dollars was Ennio Morricone's breakthrough film, but he nearly never got the assignment. Leone had wanted to use Angelo Lavagnino, who had scored *Colossus Of Rhodes*, and when the producers played Morricone's music for another Western, *Showdown In Texas* (1963), Leone hated it, thinking it sounded like watered-down Dimitri Tiomkin. When the producers insisted on a meeting, Leone and Morricone recognised each other from Trastevere, where they had spent a year in the same class at school. It was the beginning of a beautiful partnership. Morricone believes an audience can deal with only two sounds at once: so dialogue, music, and natural effects cannot all compete for attention. Watching the way Leone cuts between those elements, and intersperses music and effects seamlessly shows that the feeling was mutual.

The Not-So-Magnificent Stranger: Following the film's success, the Italian producers, Jolly Films, bought two episodes of *Rawhide*, shot some extra scenes to knit them together and released it as a film called *The Magnificent Stranger*.

Even weirder, when *A Fistful Of Dollars* was first shown on US TV, a prologue was added, where a stand-in for Eastwood was released from prison with an offer of a pardon if he 'cleaned up' San Miguel.

The Verdict: A Fistful Of Dollars still packs as much power as it did when it first came out, but it lacks the touches of a finely finished product which Leone would bring to his next three Westerns. 4/5

For A Few Dollars More (1965)

Italy/Spain/Germany

USA Distributor: United Artists (1967)

Running Times: Italy 130 mins, USA UK 128 mins

Cast: Clint Eastwood (The Man With No Name/Monco), Lee Van Cleef (Colonel Douglas Mortimer), Gian Maria Volonté (El Indio), Luigi Pistilli (Groggy), Mario Brega (Nino), Klaus Kinski (The Hunchback), Benito Stefanelli (Luke), Aldo Sambrell (Cuchillo), Josef Egger (Prophet), Mara Krup (Hotelier's Wife)

Crew: Director: Sergio Leone, Producer: Alberto Grimaldi, Script: Luciano Vincenzoni & Leone, Story: Leone & Fulvio Morsella, Dialogue: Vincenzoni, Photography: Massimo Dallamano, Music: Ennio Morricone, Conducted by Bruno Nicolai, Art Director & Costumes: Carlo Simi, Supervising Editor: Adriana Novelli, Editors: Eugenio Alabiso, Giorgio Serralonga, Assistant Director: Tonino Valerii, Titles: Luigi Lardani, Musicians: Alessandro Alessandroni (whistle, choral arrangement), I Cantori Moderni Alessandroni (choir), Bruno D'Amario Battisti (guitar)

Locations: Almería, Guadix (Spain)

Interiors: Cinecittà (Rome)

Story: Bounty killer Colonel Mortimer stops a train at Tucumari, surprises an outlaw in the bath and, using an arsenal of specialised weapons, kills him. Monco, also a bounty hunter, tracks another outlaw to a bar, kills him and three associates alerted by a corrupt sheriff. El Indio is in prison, when his men bust him out. He kills his cellmate, then proceeds to kill the man who betrayed him, but not before making him listen to his wife and child being shot. Indio times their gun duel using a musical pocket watch, which, we later learn in flashback, was taken from a woman he raped after killing her husband, who had just given it to her.

Indio's escape has pushed up the price on his head. After initially trying to drive each other out of El Paso, where each expects Indio to strike, Mortimer and Monco team up, agreeing to split the bounties on Indio and his gang. Mortimer recognises some of Indio's men in town and strikes a match on the hunchback of one of them; the hunchback's comrades stop him from retaliating. Mortimer suggests Monco should infiltrate the gang and do it by breaking another of Indio's gang out of jail. Indio accepts Monco into the gang after questioning why he did what he did. Monco's answer, that he is a bounty killer aiming to collect for all the gang, amuses Indio.

Indio robs the bank at El Paso, sending Monco with three others to create a diversion by robbing the bank at Santa Cruz. Monco kills the three and creates the diversion by forcing a telegraph operator to send a message that the bank has been robbed. Indio pulls off the robbery so successfully Mortimer and Monco have no chance to catch the gang in the planned crossfire, so Monco returns to Indio, after Mortimer grazes him with a shot along the neck, to prove he did his part.

Monco attempts to divert Indio in the opposite direction suggested by Mortimer, but Indio instead heads east to Aqua Verde, where they find Mortimer waiting for them. The hunchback seeks revenge, and after insulting him again, Mortimer kills him with a spring-loaded derringer. He tells Indio he is the man who can open the El Paso safe without damaging the money inside, and uses acid to burn through the lock. Indio then says everyone will wait until the heat from the robbery has died down before the money is split, and locks it away safely.

That night Monco sneaks in to get the money, only to find Mortimer waiting.

As they leave Mortimer reseals the strongbox. They are caught by Indio, but Monco manages to hide the loot in a tree, and Indio, checking the strongbox, assumes it is intact. They are beaten by the gang, but that night Nino sets them free, giving them their guns back, albeit empty.

Nino kills one of the band, framing another for the killing, and telling the rest that the framed man helped the gringo bounty killers escape. He sends the gang after the men, then explains to Nino that he knew they were bounty killers. Now they and his men will kill each other off, leaving the money for Indio and Nino and convincing the authorities the robbers are dead.

Monco and Mortimer reload their weapons on the edge of town. Mortimer asks that Monco leave Indio for him. They kill off the gang, while Groggy returns to Indio, killing Nino in the process. They discover the money is gone, and Groggy, realising Indio has been outfoxed, gives him an empty gun to face the gringos. As Groggy asks Indio about the musical watch, Mortimer identifies himself and calls Indio out. Groggy tosses Indio his gun belt. As Groggy tries to escape Mortimer shoots him, but Indio appears suddenly and shoots the gun from Mortimer's hand. Indio starts the watch's music for a duel, leaving Mortimer's pistol on the ground, but just as the music is about to stop, it starts again, coming this time from Mortimer's matching watch, now held by Monco. Using a rifle to keep Indio at bay, he supervises a fair gunfight within a ring; Mortimer kills Indio. Mortimer explains the woman in the watch was his sister; now that he has his revenge, Monco can keep all the bounties. Monco loads the bodies onto a wagon; and while totalling their value he realises the total is short and one is missing. He whirls and shoots Groggy who was about to kill him. On the way out of town, Monco retrieves the hold-up money from the tree.

For A Few Minutes More: The two minutes cut from the US/UK versions are significant. In the first minute, Indio baptises his gun in Holy Water (religious symbolism), and in the second minute, a flashback interrupted by Mortimer's final challenge, we see that Mortimer's sister killed herself while Indio raped her.

The Second Time Around: In the BBC's *Viva Leone* documentary Morricone described how, after *A Fistful Of Dollars*, both he and Leone knew they could do better on the next film. They did. In *For A Few Dollars More* the music box theme cues flashbacks and duels, during which the sound changes. There are bells, flamenco guitar, organ, and a trumpet playing the deguello - the 'no quarter' signal used by the Mexican army at the Alamo. Each of the three main characters received his own theme, and there were even Tiomkin-like orchestrations for Monco's entrance into Aqua Verde, and for Mortimer's riding off into the sunset, revenge accomplished. After *For A Few Dollars More*, Morricone would write most of Leone's music before filming was done. Leone actually played the themes from *Once Upon A Time In The West* on set, as directors did in the silent era, to put the actors in the mood.

A Fistful Of Motifs: The religious symbolism is continued, particularly when Indio explains his plan to rob the Bank of El Paso from the pulpit of a church (like Father Mappin in *Moby Dick*, played by Orson Welles in John Huston's 1956 film) and in terms of a parable. The family killed by Indio after he escapes from prison is a carbon copy of the 'holy' family saved by Joe in *A Fistful Of Dollars*. When Monco wants to know about Mortimer, he consults 'Prophet,' whose life has been ruined by his holdout against the railroad, a foreshadowing of *Once Upon A Time In The West*. Mortimer, by contrast, goes to the newspaper morgue to research Monco.

Indio has a model of the cabinet which hides the safe in the El Paso bank. Models will recur in later films. The music as a trigger for memory will recur in Harmonica's eponymous playing in *Once Upon A Time In The West*, and in the ringing telephone of *Once Upon A Time In America*. And Indio's drug use will be echoed in the drunken Union commander of *The Good, The Bad And The Ugly* and Noodles' opium dreams in *Once Upon A Time In America*.

Clint's rides between Indio, Santa Cruz and El Paso echo the rides in *Colossus Of Rhodes* and *A Fistful Of Dollars*. For guns in strange places we have Col. Mortimer's spring-loaded derringer up his sleeve, and Indio shooting the prison warden through the peephole of his door. We also have Monco making a dummy of himself and spinning round in a chair to kill two of Indio's gang. Finally, when Eastwood drives the wagon full of bodies off into the sunset, his hat brim is blown up by the wind, homage perhaps to Wishbone, the chuckwagon driver in *Rawhide*.

The triangular theme of *A Fistful Of Dollars* is here refined into three individuals. Eastwood remains the frontiersman-type, with Van Cleef taking over the 'Yankee' role of the Baxters and Volonté the 'Mexican' role he encapsulated in the Rojos. The climax of the film has the first of Leone's ritualistic 'bullring' shoot-outs. Mario Brega reappears as Volonté's right-hand man, a kind of Mexican Maciste, a type who will reappear as the 'Bud Spencer' characters in the Trinity movies. The pairing is at least as old as Robin Hood and Little John, and follows an established Italian film tradition of giant Buffalo and little Bill.

Call me perverse, but I see an echo of Diala, as played by Lea Massari, in Mara Krup as the hotelier's wife who gives Monco the come-on. I don't see that it serves any purpose, but I can't help but feel there's some sort of personal joke behind it. In fact, the entire check-in scene, poking fun at her midget husband, and at the customer Monco runs out of his room, is the one bit of coarse comedy that grates against the flow of the film. Originally, the two were given a bedroom scene,

41

but Leone didn't include it in the final cuts, as he previously cut a scene of Clint with a Mexican woman in *A Fistful Of Dollars*, and would cut Harmonica's scene recuperating from his wound with a whore from *Once Upon A Time In The West*. Leone's West is a masculine universe.

The Man With No Name? In *A Fistful Of Dollars,* the Clint Eastwood character is called 'Joe.' But that is always by the town's natives, who may be calling him Joe in the same way that American soldiers were always called 'Joe,' especially in the Italy of Leone's youth. Or perhaps it is 'Jo,' short for 'Joven' or kid, which is often used in Spanish.

In the English-language version of *For A Few Dollars More*, Eastwood's character is written and referred to as Monco (although some people, and many reference books, call him Manco, which may be down to simple confusion over the broad vowel sound "a" and the Gothic script on the poster where his name is seen). Monco has been interpreted to mean monk, because Eastwood wears a monklike garment but, though the religious symbolism would be nice, the Italian for monk is 'monaco' and the Spanish is 'monje'. In fact, 'monco' is the Italian for maimed or incomplete and 'monco d'un braccio' means one-armed or one-handed. Perhaps this is a play on the word single-handed or a reference to him being a lone gunman. Screenwriter Luciano Vincenzoni has confirmed this was his intention, and Eastwood seems to endorse this interpretation in the opening scene, where he does all of his punching left-handed, saving his right hand for gunplay. (Eastwood even wears a wrist gauntlet on his right hand like Burt Lancaster in *Vera Cruz*.)

References: The ritual gunfight at the end puts Lee Van Cleef in the shoes of the Randolph Scott character in Budd Boetticher's movies, a particularly apt reference since in *Ride Lonesome* (1959) Van Cleef played the villain Frank, whose long-ago killing of Ben Brigade's wife prompted Brigade's single-minded quest for revenge. Frank is forced to face Brigade in an effort to save his brother Billy, whom Brigade has bounty-hunted in anticipation of Frank's arrival. In *High Noon* Van Cleef waits for Frank Miller to rejoin his brother for his revenge on Gary Cooper's marshal.

This is a good place to put such references into context. It's important to remember here that Leone did not necessarily have those specific films in mind when planning *For A Few Dollars More*, nor even when hiring Van Cleef. Although Van Cleef seems so perfect in retrospect, he was not the first choice for *For A Few Dollars More,* and in fact he was virtually out of acting when Leone hired him. As in *A Fistful Of Dollars,* Leone envisaged Henry Fonda. Again, Fonda's agent refused to consider Spaghettis. Charles Bronson passed and Lee Marvin agreed to take the role, but then backed out to play the lead in *Cat Ballou* (1965), for which he would win an Oscar. Leone decided on Van Cleef from a picture in a directory, and from there had to locate the unemployed actor, who was scraping out a living as a painter.

But what is important is the resonance which actors like Van Cleef bring to the films, and what they inspired, visually, from Leone. Later, especially in *Once Upon A Time In The West,* Leone would deliberately evoke such referential echoes, quoting his favourite scenes and paying homage to them, but at this point I think he was seeing his story and its images refined through the prism of all the images of the Western which were ingrained in his own memory. Many of these would be brought to the surface, perhaps subconsciously, and many more would carry a meaning for the audiences, both American and European, who watched them.

Budd Boetticher: The connection between Leone and Boetticher is a fascinating one. According to Frayling, when the two met at a film festival in the late 60s, Leone greeted him by saying "Budd, dear Budd, I stole everything from you!"

The echoes of *Ride Lonesome* have already been noted, and there are plenty of other correspondences between the two men, not least in the shape of their careers. Boetticher began his Hollywood career almost by accident, when he was taken on as a technical advisor on bullfighting for Ruben Mamoulian's *Blood And Sand* (1941). He had gone to Mexico to recuperate from a football injury, and fell in love with the corrida, even studying to become a matador. He went to Hollywood and, like Leone, worked his way up as an assistant director. Unlike Leone, within three years he was directing his own features, some dozen before making *The Bullfighter And The Lady* (1951) for John Wayne's production company (John Ford lent a hand to the editing). Although he would continue to direct various B-features through the 1950s, the Wayne connection led to the first of seven Westerns starring Randolph Scott, the first and perhaps best of which, *Seven Men From Now* (1956), was produced by Wayne's Batjac company; the rest were produced by Scott and his partner, Harry Joe Brown.

These seven films, and particularly the four scripted by Burt Kennedy (one adapted from an Elmore Leonard story), are small masterpieces of the genre and, like Leone's films, repeat variations on the same basic character and plots. As Jim Kitses pointed out in his landmark study *Horizons West,* by the end of the cycle the Scott hero, usually defined by his function, like Leone's, has become absurd with no meaning except as an agent of his own vengeful agenda.

Unlike the hero, who wastes no speech, Boetticher's villains are flamboyant, often flashy, and in many of the films there is a triangle similar to Leone's trademark. In *Ride Lonesome,* for example, Scott's Ben Brigade is cooperating with Pernell Robert's (and sidekick James Coburn's) outlaws only while they take Billy to town; the outlaws assume they will face an eventual showdown with Brigade for Billy, while Brigade really is setting up the final showdown with Lee van Cleef's Frank.

The characters move through Boetticher's landscape with more direct purpose than in Leone's, where the movement is often circular. In two of the Kennedy-scripted films, the characters move from green settings to desert; in the other two the pattern is reversed. But set against the landscape, the movement and relation of the characters to each other is always the key visual aspect.

The journey in these Boetticher Westerns culminates in a showdown, which is always stylised and usually staged within some sort of ring, naturally defined rather than Leone's literal rings.

The most interesting parallel in their careers may involve where they went after their Westerns. Leone, after four ever-more intriguing Westerns, directed a fifth, *Duck, You Sucker,* which was less successful, in part because he did not particularly want to direct it, but wanted to produce and have someone else handle the directing chores. His next film, albeit a decade later, would be his gangster epic, *Once Upon A Time In America*. Boetticher made the sixth of his seven Scott Westerns specifically to get the money to direct his own gangster film, *The Rise And Fall Of Legs Diamond* (1960), which like *Once Upon A Time In America* shows an ambitious gangster eliminating his allies on his ruthless rise to the top. If you look closely at the Reginald Marsh painting used as a Coney Island poster in the station scenes of *Once Upon A Time In America,* you'll see a billing for 'Mrs. Jack 'Legs' Diamond.' After their gangster pictures, both men spent years working on personal projects: in Boetticher's case, the bullfight film *Arruza* (1972). But Boetticher returned to the Western with two films released in 1969. One was the Audie Murphy morality play *A Time For Dying*, a meditation of sorts on his 1951 Murphy vehicle, *Cimarron Kid*. The other brought the Leone connection full circle, as Clint Eastwood starred with Shirley MacLaine (as the most heavily made-up nun in the 19th century!) in Don Siegel's *Two Mules For Sister Sara*. Boetticher wrote the original script, but the finished product turned the Eastwood character into the Man With No Name.

A Metaphysical Conundrum: Indio uses his musical watch as a countdown for his duels. His instruction, "when you hear the music finish, begin," is absurd: how can you hear when something stops? This obviously gives Indio a huge advantage in any duel, but I suppose you'd have to be an even braver fool to argue the point with him.

The Verdict: For A Few Dollars More is the most tightly constructed of the Dollars films. The characters are finely balanced, and the power of both Leone's edits, the flashbacks and Morricone's score are intensified by their relative underuse. There are a number of scenes of individual brilliance, particularly the introductions of all three characters, Eastwood's entrance into Aqua Verde, Van Cleef's encounters with the hunchbacked Kinski and the final shoot-out. This is Leone's equivalent to a Budd Boetticher film; a tightly formal restating of the genre. 5/5

The Good, The Bad And The Ugly (1966)

Working Title: The Two Magnificent Tramps

Italy/USA (United Artists 1968)

Running Times: Italy 180 mins, France 166 mins, USA 161 mins, UK 148 mins

Cast: Clint Eastwood (Blondie, The Good), Lee Van Cleef (Angel Eyes, The Bad), Eli Wallach (Tuco, The Ugly), Aldo Giuffre (Union Commander), Luigi Pistilli (Father Ramirez), Rada Rassimov (Maria), Mario Brega (Corporal Wallace), Antonio Casale (Jackson/Bill Carson), Al Mulloch (One-Armed Gunman), John Bartha (Sheriff), Enzo Petito (Gunsmith), Angelo Novi (Monk), Lorenzo Robledo (Clem), Benito Steffanelli, Claudio Scarchilli, Sandro Scarchilli, Aldo Sambrell (Angel Eyes' gang), Antonio Casas (Stevens), Chelo Alonso (Stevens' wife), Antonio Ruiz (Youngest Son)

Crew: Director: Sergio Leone, Producer: Alberto Grimaldi, Script: Luciano Vincenzoni, Leone, Age Scarpelli (aka Agenore Incrocci & Furio Scarpelli), Sergio Donati (Uncredited), Story: Vincenzoni & Leone, English Dialogue: Mickey Knox, Photography: Tonino Delli Colli, Music: Ennio Morricone, Conducted by Bruno Nicolai, Editors: Nino Baragli, Eugenio Alabiso, Art Director, Sets & Costumes: Carlo Simi, Assistant Director: Giancarlo Santi, Stunts: Benito Stefanelli, Titles: Luigi Lardani, Musicians: Alessandro Alessandroni (whistling, vocals), Bruno D'Amario Battisti (guitar), Franco DeGemini (harmonica), I Cantori Moderni di Alessandroni (choir), E Wolf Ferrari, I Cammarota, F Catania, Michele Lacerenza (trumpets), E Gioieni, F Cosacchi, G Spagnolo, Edda Dell'Orso (vocals)

Locations: Almería, Colemanari, Burgos (Spain)

Interiors: Elios Film (Rome)

Story: Texas, during the Civil War. We meet the three main characters in a series of vignettes, each of which ends on a freeze frame identifying them with a graphic. Bounty hunters enter a cantina, and after shooting them dead, Tuco explodes through a glass window, still gnawing a joint of meat. 'The Ugly.' Angel Eyes has been hired to kill Stevens and get information about Bill Carson from him. He conveys the information to his employer, gets a lead on Carson then kills him, finishing the job Stevens 'hired' him to do in his desperation. 'The Bad.' Tuco is saved from three more bounty hunters by Blondie, who turns him in himself, only to shoot the rope away as Tuco is being hung. They go into business collecting bounties, but after arguing about the split, Blondie seeks out bigger pay days, and abandons Tuco in the desert. 'The Good!'

Tuco survives the desert, captures Blondie and is about to hang him when an exploding cannon shell saves Blondie. Meanwhile, Angel Eyes has learnt the complete story of Bill Carson's stolen Confederate gold from Shorty, a legless Confederate veteran, and that the eyepatched

Carson frequents a whore named Maria. Angel Eyes tracks down Maria and, beating her, learns Carson has re-enlisted.

Tuco tracks Blondie and recaptures him just as he is about to shoot the noose from his new partner, also called Shorty, whom Tuco lets hang. He leads Blondie into the desert and is again about to kill him when a Confederate carriage appears. On board is 'Bill Carson' who trades information about the gold for water, telling Tuco the gold is buried in a cemetery, but when Tuco leaves for water Carson tells Blondie the name on the gravestone. Tuco and Blondie are once again partners. Taking the dead soldiers' uniforms (and Carson's eyepatch) Tuco brings Blondie to a monastery being used as a hospital. Tuco's brother is the head of the order and has just returned from their father's funeral. They argue and Tuco hits his brother. As he rides away with Blondie he explains how close he and his brother are. Blondie hands him a cigar, showing sympathy for the first time. Tuco and Blondie are captured by Union soldiers after Tuco, mistaking their dust-covered uniforms for grey, has pretended to be Confederate. They are taken to Betterville POW camp, where Angel Eyes is now a sergeant. Despite their mutual recognition, Tuco answers to the name Bill Carson and, when tortured by Angel Eyes' assistant, Wallace, finally reveals the name of the cemetery. Angel Eyes realises torturing Blondie for the remaining detail would not work, so they agree a partnership. Tuco escapes from Wallace and follows refugees to a town, where he bathes in a ruined hotel. He has been recognised, but kills the man who confronts him in the bathtub. Blondie, recognising the sound of Tuco's gun, wanders away from Angel Eyes' men and kills the one who follows him. He and Tuco reform their partnership and kill Angel Eyes' henchmen. But Angel Eyes has already escaped.

Blondie and Tuco find their way to the cemetery blocked by a pointless and endless battle over the Langstone bridge. The drunken Union commander has a plan to blow up the bridge during the truce following an attack, but dares not disobey orders. He is wounded in the next attack; Tuco and Blondie, having exchanged their secret information (Tuco telling Blondie the cemetery, Blondie revealing the name on the grave), blow up the bridge. As it blows, the captain dies happy, ending his agony of sending men to their useless deaths. On the other side of the river, Blondie comforts a dying Confederate soldier, placing his jacket over him. Tuco takes a horse and rides away. Blondie, taking a folded blanket from under the soldier's head, uses a cannon to bring Tuco down, but Tuco discovers he is already in Sad Hill cemetery. Tuco searches for the grave of Arch Stanton, the name Blondie has given him, and starts to dig for gold. Blondie interrupts to toss him a shovel, and when the camera pans up to him we see him wearing the blanket, in the 'Man With No Name' identity.

Angel Eyes appears, tossing another shovel, and telling Blondie to start digging too. But the grave contains only a skeleton - Blondie has given Tuco the wrong name. He writes the correct name on a rock, which he places in the centre of the circle in the middle of the graveyard. The three gunmen form a triangle within a circle. Angel Eyes goes for his gun first and is shot by Blondie. Tuco fires at Blondie, but discovers Blondie emptied his gun the night before. Tuco digs up the treasure, only to discover Blondie has fashioned a noose for him. Blondie stands Tuco on a cross, puts the noose around his neck and rides away, leaving him half the gold. On a far-off rise, Blondie stops, aims a rifle at Tuco. He shoots the rope, then rides off as Tuco shouts abuse at him.

Money Talks, Clint Nearly Walks: The Good, The Bad And The Ugly was Leone's first big-budget operation and it shows. United Artists put up half a million dollars in advance, in return for half the foreign sales, but a good part of the budget was taken up by Eastwood's fee. Having been paid $15,000 for *A Fistful Of Dollars* (out of a budget of $200,000), and $50,000 and a small percentage for *For A Few Dollars More* (out of $600,000), Clint's fee for *The Good, The Bad And The Ugly* was a quarter of a million dollars, plus 10% of the profits. The total budget for the film was about $1,300,000. Clint knew Leone had to have him, especially for the US market, and the fact he had Leone over a barrel appears the have been the real start of the cooling of relations between the star and the director. By the time Eastwood was due to dub his lines, having seen his part reduced considerably in the face of Eli Wallach's bravura performance and Leone's fondness for the Tuco character, Eastwood had to be pressured to break his schedule and complete the dubbing. He originally insisted it be done to the original script, rather than the final shooting script. Depending on which story you believe, either he was coerced into working by threats from United Artists' Chris Mankiewicz, and the dubbing was supervised by Leone and Sergio Donati, or Leone had departed and it was supervised by Mickey Knox.

Knox was an actor who had moved to Europe when he was blacklisted in 1950s Hollywood, and was a good friend of Wallach's. In fact, he would act as executive producer on the best of the three other Spaghetti Westerns Wallach would make, Duccio Tessari's many-titled *Don't Turn The Other Cheek* (1971), a cross between *Sister Sara* and *Duck, You Sucker* which co-starred Franco Nero and Lynn Redgrave! On *The Good, The Bad And The Ugly* and again on *Once Upon A Time In The West* he was responsible for the English dialogue, working from the original script. He must have added something in the translation, because the English seems far crisper, the lines more telling, than they did in the first two Westerns.

Eastwood eventually fell out with Leone and refused to reprise his Dollars' role one last time in Leone's proposed killing off of the three *The Good, The Bad And The Ugly* characters at the start of *Once Upon A Time In The West* (both Lee Van Cleef and Eli Wallach had agreed). They argued in interviews about exactly who created the Man With No Name, who bought the cigars and the wardrobe, who conceived the strong silent nature of the character. In later years, the two reconciled, and last were together for the Rome premiere of Eastwood's *Bird*. The end credits of *Unforgiven* begin 'To Sergio and Don.' (Don referred to director Don Siegel, who essentially mentored Eastwood's directing career.)

A Fistful Of Motifs: The triangle of main characters recurs, again with the 'civilised' gringo, the 'frontiersman' and the Mexican peon. Unlike *For A Few Dollars More,* this time the three-way shoot-out at the end is literally three-way. Religious symbolism is toned down, though the most is made of the final shoot-out in consecrated ground, and Tuco standing on a gravestone cross. But Tuco visits his brother, a priest, in one of the most sentimental and moving scenes in all Leone's cinema. His arguments with and contempt for his brother are overheard by Blondie, unknown to Tuco, who then describes the mutual love of their reunion to Blondie with no irony.

The bridge bearing the name Langstone recalls Sisyphus and his never-ending battle to roll a stone uphill. The Union commander complains that the battle, echoing World War I trench warfare, is useless and never-ending.

Guns In Strange Places: Tuco shoots a one-armed gunman looking for revenge with a gun kept under the water while he bathes (and utters the classic line: "When you have to shoot, shoot! Don't talk!").

Forty Guns Again: We've already discussed the impact of Sam Fuller on Leone, but we should note that *Forty Guns* is also one of the all-time great dust movies. The opening sequence (which Leone and Valerii would parody in *My Name Is Nobody)* where Barbara Stanwyck and her 40 guns gallop past Griff and his brothers in their wagon is echoed in the dusty cavalry scene where Confederate horsemen become Union by shaking off their dust. Bertolucci once said what he loved about Leone was that he showed the rear end of horses, and in that same sequence Fuller shoots from underneath the back of the wagon, through the horse's rear, as the riders go past. Characters with names like Blondie and Tuco recall Fuller's films (Griff seems to be his idea of a hero's common name) and the list of characters sometimes sounds like the bark of guns: Griff and Brock. Finally, Rod Steiger, who would play a Mexican in *Duck, You Sucker* plays an Irish Confederate Indian in Fuller's *Run Of The Arrow* (1957).

Men At War: Although the triangle of the three main characters echoes *For A Few Dollars More*, they act out their story on a much wider landscape. The Civil War, ostensibly in the background, is actually in the forefront of Leone's filming. Oddly enough, the West of Western movies is usually that of the post-Civil War period and few films have been made about the War itself, though the excellent *Glory* (1989) and Ted Turner's 1993 made-for-TV fake-beard epic *Gettysburg* stand as recent exceptions to that rule. No less a personage than Orson Welles was to warn Leone that Civil War movies were box-office poison!

Leone's portrayal of the Civil War is exceptional. Generally considered the first modern war, the Civil War produced unheard-of levels of carnage, as military tactics struggled to compete with technical advances like rifled muskets, repeating weapons and rail transport. The scenes at the bridge, where the Union commander drinks himself into forgetfulness while sending men to die in a Sisyphean dance with his enemy, are as bleak as any drama of the trenches.

Leone pulls no punches in his portrayal of the conditions in the prisoner of war camp—the notorious Andersonville, South Carolina, is the model and referred to specifically by the Union commander. His Betterville also echoes the concentration camps, with the ostensible aim of betterment (arbeit macht frei), and most powerfully, the prison orchestra that plays while Angel Eyes has Wallace torture Tuco.

With the historical background moved to the forefront, the main characters are reduced somewhat, particularly since Eastwood and Van Cleef fade in the face of Eli Wallach's exuberant performance as Tuco. Leone claimed it was not Wallach's role as the bandit chief in *The Magnificent Seven* which he had in mind when he cast him as Tuco, but rather for his portrayal of a bandit in *How The West Was Won*, where his menace was touched with a certain psychotic humour. The physical brilliance of Wallach's playing: his maintaining Tuco's rat-like demeanour and the almost constant exaggeration of motions are in sharp contrast to the more static Eastwood and the tightly controlled Van Cleef. Leone continued to cast 'method' actors (Jason Robards, Rod Steiger) opposite strong 'natural' actors (Charles Bronson, James Coburn).

The Stock Company: With Tonino Delli Colli replacing Massimo Dallamano as director of photography, Leone's stock company was complete. In addition to Morricone, it included art director Carlo Simi, editor Nino Baragli, stunt director Benito Stefanelli and assistant director Giancarlo Santi. For the Dollars films, the group included Luigi Lardani, who devised the titles. On *The Good, The Bad And The Ugly* it was his idea to freeze the frames on the introduction of each character. Such a unit not only work better together, because of their long familiarity with each others' foibles, but also know the previous work intimately, so they all understand what works and what doesn't, and what references are being made to earlier films. They share, as it were, the same learning curve.

To that group might be added screenwriters Luciano Vincenzoni and Sergio Donati - Leone's equivalent to Ford's Dudley Nichols and Frank Nugent. Vincenzoni was a relatively prestigious writer, whose contacts in Europe got Leone his first US distribution deal with United Artists. While paying homage to Leone's instinctive talents as a 'natural' film-maker (perhaps another sign of that north/south divide in Italian culture), Vincenzoni also referred to writing the Westerns with one hand, as hack work, which may account for some of the playfulness in his approach. It was Vincenzoni who sold the basic idea of *The Good, The Bad And The Ugly* - three rogues chasing treasure in the Civil War - to United Artists, and who eventually came up with the title. He saw the film in terms of Mario Monicelli's *The Great War* (1959), which United Artists had distributed, so the powerful allegories to World War I in the prison and bridge scenes originated with him. Leone brought in the team of Age Scarpelli to inject some humour, but little of their dialogue remains. Instead, Sergio Donati came in to script doctor, especially when Leone found himself having to make big cuts to bring the running time down. Because Leone preferred to cut entire sequences, rather than trim the rhythm of others, Donati had to write brand new dialogue to return information cut from the film. He would go uncredited, but would be credited on *Once Upon A Time In The West*. Leone was notoriously reluctant to share the creative credit with his writers, which is not unusual. But Vincenzoni, because of his influence in bringing UA on board, also had a percentage of the profits; so almost inevitably he and Leone began feuding. He would come back crucially, however, to script *Duck, You Sucker*.

He's Good Bad, But He's Not Evil: What makes 'Il Buono' actually 'good'? This is a crucial question. The primary answer is that Leone is trying to dissolve the Western's preconception of good and evil. We understand instinctively that Blondie, while not good in the classic pure hero sense, is also not evil in the sense that Angel Eyes transcends mere 'badness.' Still, Blondie, the character identified as 'the good,' is introduced in a scene where he double-crosses his partner and leaves him alone, on foot, hands bound, some 70 miles into the desert.

With that in mind I believe we can read *The Good, The Bad And The Ugly* as a prequel to the Man With No Name films, explaining how the Joe Monco character was formed. His progress through the film is to learn both sympathy and compassion: the first when he begins to appreciate Tuco's sensitivity (after hearing him confronting his brother and then lying about their fraternal love afterwards) and courage (in revenging himself on his torturers). His compassion as a killer is brought out by the senselessness of the Civil War and inspires two acts. The first is the blowing-up of the bridge, to put an end to the Union commander's agony of sending his men to die uselessly. Immediately after that, on the other side of the river, Blondie comforts a dying Confederate, giving him his jacket and, when he leaves, taking a blanket that becomes his poncho. All of sudden, he is the Man With No Name in the costume we recognise, and he gives the poncho his stylised flip in case we miss the point.

From this point, however, we can understand the cryptic reference he makes to Marisol in *A Fistful Of Dollars*, about not being able to help. And it also puts a different light on the character of Colonel Mortimer in *For A Few Dollars More,* with whom Monco has the running 'old man/

boy' verbal duel. Perhaps Mortimer reminds him of another older man, one not so straightforward, whom he encountered in the Civil War? Or more likely, Leone was just playing with stereotypes, never knowing decades later someone would try to piece together an eschatology for his genre characters!

Changing Sides: The on/off partnership between Tuco and Blondie is only one of many instances of allegiances not being what they seem. At the start of the film Angel Eyes turns on the man who hired him to track down Jackson and kill Stevens, just as Blondie will turn on him when Tuco returns after killing Wallace.

Even the allegiances of the Civil War are murky: Tuco welcomes a troop of Confederate cavalry only to discover their grey uniforms are really dusty Union blue. Angel Eyes seems able to join the Union army as a sergeant and then leave it at will. A hotel owner cynically cheers on both sides while watching the Confederates pull out of town. (Is that Leone favourite Joseph Egged as General Sibley in the procession?) The Union commander at the bridge wants to disobey his orders and blow up the bridge so the two sides will have nothing to fight over. Blondie comforts the Union commander and then a Confederate on opposite sides of the river which divides them. The war, in all its horror, makes a sharp contrast between Leone's three protagonists. They kill for specific reasons; the men in war appear to be dying for no rational purpose, except dying itself.

The Verdict: Critic Michael Goldfarb called *The Good, The Bad And The Ugly* the perfect pulp film. Leone expands the scale of his picture without losing the focus of *For A Few Dollars More*. Morricone exceeds himself with the score and the final shoot-out is one that no one has matched in more than three decades. It rarely gets any better than this. 5/5

A Screenful Of Spaghetti

A Fistful Of Dollars was by no means the first Spaghetti Western, but its success opened a veritable floodgate of production, as the Italian film industry began another of the cycles of genre boom and bust like the peplum movies. In the next decade, some 400-500 Spaghetti Westerns were produced. Although American critics originally intended the term as derisory, in retrospect it seems particularly apt, conveying something of the incredibly offbeat variety of Westerns which a generation of film-makers trained in the Cinecittà production line produced.

European Westerns were already being shot by German, Spanish and Italian companies, often co-productions between the three. Adaptations of novels by the German Western writer Karl May had been extremely popular in Europe, with American stars like Lex Barker and Stewart Granger playing May's hero, Old Shatterhand, and with the Germans shooting in Yugoslavia. Spanish/Italian Westerns like *Gunfight At High Noon* (1963) (starring Richard Harrison, who would originally be suggested to Leone as the lead in *A Fistful Of Dollars), Ride And Kill* (1963) and *Buffalo Bill, Hero of the Far West* (1964) (starring Gordon Scott and photographed by Massimo Dallamano/'Jack Dalmas') were shot in Spain.

In the wake of *A Fistful Of Dollars,* the Cinecittà film-makers rushed to get Westerns into production, and the market was soon filled with a series of Men With Odd Names: Djangos, Ringos, Sabatas, Sartanas and the like.

Leone's old collaborator, Sergio Corbucci, who had seen the possibilities for shooting Westerns while working on *The Last Days Of Pompeii,* got the ball rolling with his 1964 Western *Minnesota Clay,* starring Cameron Mitchell. It was notable for being the first where the crew were credited with their own, Italian, names. Corbucci quickly followed with four films in the next two years, of which *Django* (1966) is the most memorable. Comparing it to the 'finest and polished' Westerns of Leone, Geoffrey O'Brien described it as, 'a rotgut little bloodbath,' and that it, 'gives a better sense of how the Italians drove a stake through the heart of Tom Mix.' It opens with Franco Nero's Django dragging a coffin across the desert landscape. The coffin, and the cemetery shoot-out, would recall motifs from *A Fistful Of Dollars;*

the coffin's contents were reprised by Dennis Hopper's Vietnam veteran in James Toback's arty *Tracks* (1976). Corbucci also directed Joseph Cotton in *The Hellbenders* (1966) and a young Burt Reynolds in *Navajo Joe* (1966), where Reynolds did a dry run for his *Deliverance* (1972) persona.

The fourth of Corbucci's 1966 releases was *Ringo's Golden Pistol*, a follow-up to the two Ringo films made the year before by Duccio Tessari, with Giuliano Gemma in the title role. In general, Spaghettis can be placed into a few categories, and in a sense Leone's films can be seen as the apotheosis of those categories. The most common plots are: the lone stranger riding into a hostile or divided town (à la *A Fistful Of Dollars*); the revenge or treasure hunt (à la *For A Few Dollars More, The Good, The Bad And The Ugly, Once Upon A Time In The West*); the revolution (usually with a European professional contrasted against a Mexican peasant, à la *Duck, You Sucker*); or variations on the theme played for comic value.

The number varies from source to source, but in the peak years of 1966 through 1968 there were close to 200 Italian Westerns. One of the most interesting was Damiano Damiani's *Quien Sabe?* (literally 'Who Knows?' better known in English as *A Bullet For The General*), which began a cycle of overtly political themes, pairing Gian Maria Volonté's Mexican with Lou Castel's (Luigi Castellato) gringo. It was scripted by Franco Solinas, who wrote Pontecorvo's *Battle Of Algiers* and, more apropos, *Queimada* (aka *Burn!*).

Lee van Cleef became a major star, first in Sergio Sollima's *The Big Gundown* (1966), and playing his Mortimer character as the unlikely-named Sabata, a former Confederate officer with a high-tech armoury right out of TV's *The Wild, Wild West*.

With Dan Duryea and Henry Silva starring in Carlo Lizzani's *Un Fiume Di Dollari* (*A River of Dollars*, 1966), better known in English as *The Hills Run Red*, it was as if the 1950s B-Westerns had come back to life in Italy.

Lizzani would return in 1967 with *Requiescant*, with a cast including Piers Paolo Pasolini as a gun-toting padre. Sollima would make *Face To Face* (1967), an offbeat and original film co-scripted with Sergio Donati, in which Gian Maria Volonté plays an Ivy League-type professor sent to the southwest to fight his tuberculosis (shades of Doc Holliday), where he becomes involved with a half-breed outlaw leader (Tomas Milian, a Cuban-born actor who played in Visconti's *Boccaccio*

70 (1962) and *The Leopard* (1963)) and eventually, abandoning his pretence of academic interest in the behaviour of bandits, becomes a vicious outlaw himself.

Corbucci would take another political story by Solinas, which was also scripted by Luciano Vincenzoni, and make *A Professional Gun* (1968). This was a sort of precursor for *Duck, You Sucker*. He would also make *The Great Silence* (1968) with Jean-Louis Trintignant and Klaus Kinski, whose final sequences in the snow recall André De Toth's magnificent *Day Of The Outlaw* (1959). By now, big names were flocking to Italy: Robert Ryan and Arthur Kennedy starred in Franco Giraldi's *Dead Or Alive* (1967); John Ireland played with Milian in Sergio Sollima's *Run Man Run* (1968); even Gilbert Roland in Bruno Corbucci's restaging of *Hamlet*, *The Dirty Story Of The West* (1968).

The bubble would soon burst. The genre descended into films designed to showcase pop stars like Johnny Hallyday or Robert Charlebois, and Enzo Barboni would have the greatest box-office success of all the Spaghetti directors by pairing Terence Hill (Mario Girotti) and Bud Spencer (Carlo Pedersoli) in the comic Trinity series. Leone parodied this in *My Name Is Nobody*.

It's impossible to convey the full breadth of the Spaghetti Western explosion. While enjoying their creativity, their sense of experimentation and their grappling with timely themes, it is also readily apparent to even a casual viewer that there is a great qualitative gap between them and Leone's Westerns as they quickly evolved from *A Fistful Of Dollars*. This gap may be explained primarily by the unity of Leone's own sense of the Western as fairy tale, which was primarily a visual one derived from Westerns themselves. For most of the makers of Spaghettis, the boom in the genre provided an opportunity to make films; for Leone, from the start, Westerns were the thing he wanted to make.

Many directors took interesting storylines and grafted them onto Western settings. Many directed rousing action sequences. Some tried to match the slower pacing and extreme close-ups for the effects Leone produced. But the elements rarely hold together in such a unified fashion. Here we see the importance of the detail in Leone's sets and costume, of the tightly controlled stage on which his characters move, even in open spaces. We realise that the rhythms of his films are just as tightly controlled. Ennio Morricone did scores for many other Spaghetti

Westerns, but never do they have the effect of his Leone music, because it is not integrated in the same fashion into the heartbeat of the film.

Leone acted in one Spaghetti Western, playing a gruff hotel clerk in *Cemetery Without Crosses* (1967) directed by the French actor Robert Hossein, who starred in it and dedicated the film to Leone. Somewhat parodic itself (featuring a villain named Will Rogers!) Leone's scene recalled the hotel scene from *For A Few Dollars More*. Interestingly, the film was co-scripted by a young film critic, Dario Argento, and drew heavily on Nicholas Ray's *Johnny Guitar* (1954). For his next film, Leone wanted to extend the boundaries of his Western work, into the epic, and he would call on Argento and another struggling young film-maker, Bernardo Bertolucci, for a script. Again influenced by *Johnny Guitar*, they would come up with the story that became *Once Upon A Time In The West*.

Once Upon A Time In The West (1968)

Italy/USA (Paramount)

Running Times: Italy 168 mins, US UK 144 mins

Cast: Claudia Cardinale (Jill McBain), Henry Fonda (Frank), Jason Robards (Cheyenne), Charles Bronson (Harmonica), Gabriele Ferzetti (Morton), Paulo Stoppa (Sam), Woody Strode (Stony), Jack Elam (Snaky), Keenan Wynn (Sheriff), Marco Zuanelli (Wobbles), Frank Wolff (McBain), Lionel Stander (Trading-post owner), Spartaco Conversi (shot through boot), Claudio Mancini (Harmonica's brother), Enzo Santaniello (Timmy McBain), Simonetta Santaniello (Maureen McBain), Benito Stefanelli, Fabio Testi

Uncredited: Luana Strode (Indian woman), Al Muloch (Knuckles), Dino Mele (young Harmonica)

Crew: Director: Sergio Leone, Executive Producer: Fulvio Morsella, Producer: Bino Cicogna, Script: Sergio Donati & Leone, Story: Bernardo Bertolucci, Dario Argento & Leone, English Dialogue: Mickey Knox, Photography: Tonino Delli Colli, Music: Ennio Morricone, Conducted by Morricone, Art Director, Sets & Costumes: Carlo Simi, Editor: Nino Baragli, Assistant Director: Giancarlo Santi, Stunts: Benito Stefanelli, Musicians: Franco DeGemini (harmonica), Alessandro Alessandroni (whistling), Edda Dell'Orso (vocals)

Locations: Monument Valley (Arizona and Utah), Alameira, Guadix (Spain)

Interiors: Cinecittà, Luce (Rome)

Story: Harmonica, expecting to meet Frank at a deserted train station, is met by three of Frank's men, whom he is forced to kill, getting slightly wounded himself. As McBain and his children prepare a welcome meal for his prospective bride, also arriving by train, they are massacred by riders in dusters: Frank shoots the young boy after one of his men says his name. When no one meets Jill, arriving in Flagstone from New Orleans, she hires a buggy to take her to McBain's Sweetwater, learning that, contrary to McBain's promises of fortune, it is worthless desert.

The buggy stops at a trading post, where a flurry of shooting outside announces the entrance of Cheyenne, still handcuffed. Cheyenne encounters Harmonica at the end of the bar. Cheyenne's gang arrive late, dressed in their trademark dusters, but Harmonica learns they're not connected to the men he killed at the station.

Arriving at Sweetwater in mid-funeral, Jill reveals she is Mrs McBain, having already been married in New Orleans. A piece of duster found nailed to a door is evidence Cheyenne's gang murdered the family. Jill searches for a sign of the wealth that McBain promised her. In town, Harmonica confronts Wobbles, who'd set up the meeting with Frank, telling him he knows Frank killed the McBains and framed Cheyenne. Meanwhile, as Jill searches for McBain's hidden fortune, she finds only a model of a train station. Cheyenne shows up, explaining to her he's been framed for the murders of her family, but he doesn't know why.

Reporting back to the crippled railroad boss Mr Morton, who only wanted the McBains scared, Frank says "people scare better when they're dying." Morton's dream is to see the Pacific Ocean from his train. As Jill is about to leave the farm, she finds Harmonica in the barn. He strips the finery off her dress and follows her to the well, where he kills two of Frank's men before they can drive her off. Cheyenne and his men, still in range of the house, were prepared to do the same.

Harmonica sends Jill to have Wobbles set up a meeting with Frank, then follows him to Morton's train. Frank sees Harmonica's shadow on top of the car and takes him prisoner. He pushes Wobbles off the train, and before Wobbles can warn him that Cheyenne is underneath the carriage, Frank kills Wobbles. Frank asks Harmonica who he is, and Harmonica answers with the names of men Frank has killed. Learning that the men he sent to McBain's are dead, Frank heads off to take care of Jill himself. Cheyenne frees Harmonica, but leaves Morton alive.

In Flagstone, Jill has taken a huge delivery of building materials paid for by McBain, and when she sees a specially cut sign, she recognises it as a station and realises McBain's plan. Back at Sweetwater, she searches for the model, only to find Frank already holding it. Morton goes to Frank's hideout (in a cave) where he is holding Jill, to stop him from killing her. After sleeping with her, Frank comes up with another plan.

Meanwhile, Harmonica explains to Cheyenne that McBain's deal with the railroad includes a clause saying he loses his rights if a station isn't built by the time the rails reach Sweetwater. Cheyenne gets his men started on the building.

Frank forces Jill to auction her land and his men prevent bidders. But Harmonica wins the bidding at $5.000, turning in Cheyenne for his bounty to get the cash. Instead of putting him in jail, the sheriff surprises Cheyenne by putting him on board Morton's train, for Yuma. On board the train, Morton has bribed Frank's men to turn against him.

Harmonica refuses Frank's offer of $5,001 for the land, while watching Frank's men take positions to ambush him. He twice saves Frank's life, later explaining to Jill "I didn't let THEM kill him—it's not the same thing." Frank returns to the train, finding Cheyenne's men and his dead, and Morton dying by a puddle of water. Cheyenne, wounded, arrives back at McBain's. Frank arrives for a final showdown with Harmonica. Harmonica's flashback comes into focus, revealing Frank putting a harmonica between the lips of a young boy, on whose shoulders his brother is being hanged. When the boy collapses, his brother dies. Harmonica kills Frank and, before Frank dies, puts the harmonica in his mouth.

Harmonica, as Cheyenne has predicted to Jill, leaves. Cheyenne follows, wounded more seriously than it appeared. He falls off his horse, explaining that he was shot by "Mr Choo Choo." He dies, his music replaced by the blast of a train whistle. Jill's music rises and she takes water down to a newly arrived group of workers. Harmonica rides off with Cheyenne's body.

Birth Of A Screenplay: Bernardo Bertolucci had called Ray's *Johnny Guitar* the first 'baroque' Western, which is interesting because many critics since have referred to Leone as initiating the Western's baroque period, implying the eventual death of the genre. Bertolucci had already made *Before The Revolution* (1964), but couldn't get another directing assignment, when he went to the first showing of *The Good, The Bad And The Ugly* and met Leone and Argento in the projection room. Leone commissioned the two budding film-makers to write the original treatment for *Once Upon A Time In The West*.

Bertolucci convinced Leone about parts of the story by making allusions to the American Westerns Leone loved, but found the hardest part was getting Leone to accept female characters. One such scene, of Harmonica in a whorehouse, would be cut from the film. Bertolucci's scene of the McBain's massacre survived, complete with sound of cicadas. Argento was responsible for Jack Elam's fly. Leone did have a knack for spotting talent, both Bertolucci and Argento would go to huge international success. When shooting began, however, Leone called on Sergio Donati to join him in Spain and write new material as he tried to shorten the picture.

A Fistful Of Motifs: Religious imagery again: the burial of the McBains, Jill finding McBain's widow's rosary, Cheyenne saying killing a kid would be like killing a priest. Harmonica's brother is hung from what appears to be a church bell on the gate of a churchyard. Cheyenne accuses Harmonica of being a Judas when he's turned in for the reward (although it appears to be a plan the two have worked out in advance).

McBain's model of the station and town recalls Indio's model safe. Both recall the model kept by Joan Crawford in Nicholas Ray's *Johnny Guitar*, who intends to corner the market in land for development as the railroad arrives.

The final shoot-out is staged within a large circle, an impromptu corral. There are only the two duellists, but Fonda and the camera circle a stationary Bronson. Frank is the character whose motivations have swung in various directions, while Harmonica has had only the single, straightforward motivation from the start.

Harmonica's eponymous instrument is like Indio's watch, in that its notes can cue flashbacks, but also serves to define his character, both musically and in terms of a life devoted solely to revenge.

Morton's very name, like Mortimer's, suggests death (morte), and greed (More-ton). Frank, meanwhile, is always frank, especially with Morton.

Guns In Strange Places: In a marvellous visual scene, Cheyenne shoots one of Frank's men through his boot, which appears to be climbing down into the railway car. Morton avoids being shot in that scene by spinning his swivel chair, the reverse of Eastwood's move in *For A Few Dollars More*.

References: Leone described *Once Upon A Time In The West* as being filled with "quotes from the films I love." It's easy to spot moments from John Sturges' *Magnificent Seven*, Robert Aldrich's *Last*

Sunset, Samuel Fuller's *Run Of The Arrow*, Fritz Lang's *Western Union* (1941), John Ford's *Iron Horse* (1924), among many others.

The major references are to *Johnny Guitar*. Some have already been noted above, but also in the more obvious sense, that Sterling Hayden, like Harmonica, is identified by his eponymous instrument and turns out to have a past closely connected to one of the main characters. The story of *Johnny Guitar* also concerns a woman trying to keep real estate that will become valuable when the railroad finally arrives. As in *Once Upon A Time In The West,* the real villains try to blame the crimes on someone else. Johnny, like Harmonica, often sits by knowingly while the action seems to take place around him. Nicholas Ray was crucial for European critics for the way he twisted standard genre elements into a wonderfully stylised personal vision, which could serve as a decent enough definition of Leone as well.

Leone seems to show the epic nature of *Once Upon A Time In The West* with repeated references to John Ford, particularly in the use of Monument Valley. Also, the scenes of railway building recall Ford's silent *Iron Horse*, and the use of Woody Strode in the opening scene recalls a number of Ford pictures.

Ford's *The Man Who Shot Liberty Valence* is about gunfighter help being necessary to let civilisation proceed. And that was the film where Jimmy Stewart made his famous comment about legend replacing fact, which is a statement we had seen before in Ford, specifically in *Fort Apache* (1948), where John Wayne, as Colonel Yorke, does nothing to disabuse the reporter who has forgotten the brave Major Collingwood and who has helped make the undeserving Colonel Thursday into a national hero. The cold and ruthless Thursday was played by Henry Fonda, who was well known for his heroic, honest, decent roles.

Fonda was uneasy about what he would do with the totally evil Frank. He arrived on set with brown contact lenses, which Leone made him throw away. Not until his character had led the massacre of a family, and he had shot down a frightened boy who stood frozen before him, and Leone brought the camera in for a close-up of his eyes, did Fonda see what Leone was after. The shot which places the audience in exactly the same position as the murdered boy is laced with shock: the eyes are deep pure blue and they belong to Henry Fonda! As a villain!

The equally famous opening scene at the train station recalls the station scenes in *High Noon,* a reference made more specific by the presence of Jack Elam, who played the drunk in Gary Cooper's cell.

The scene took four days to shoot, with three hours spent simply getting the drop of water on Woody Strode's head. After experimenting with prop flies, they actually got Jack Elam's fly sequence with the first insect they used, by daubing marmalade on Elam's cheeks.

Frank's walk through Flagstone with his former henchmen trying to kill him recalls Cooper's final gunfight in *High Noon*, particularly with the painted clock face (without hands) behind which a gunman lurks.

A number of the movie's best lines are lifted from other films. Frank's dismissal of Wobbles, who wears both a belt and suspenders (braces), "how can you trust a man who can't even trust his own pants?" comes from Billy Wilder's *Ace In The Hole* (1951). Cheyenne says "Go away, I don't want you to see me die" to Harmonica, echoing Joel McCrea to Randolph Scott at the end of *Ride The High Country*. Cheyenne's description of being shot by Morton "when they do you in, pray it's someone who knows WHERE to shoot," also echoes McCrea's description of his wounds in that same scene.

Tragedy On Set: Al Muloch, who played Knuckles, the third of Frank's gang gunned down by Harmonica at the start of the film, committed suicide by throwing himself out of the window of his hotel bedroom in his Western costume. Leone, worried his shooting of the scene wasn't complete, was concerned to get the costume back in case he needed to use a stand-in.

During the Flagstone shoot-out sequence, one of the stuntmen was seriously injured falling badly from a roof. Fabio Testi survived, but got out of stunts and into acting, becoming a major star in Italy.

The Verdict: For some, *Once Upon A Time In The West* is the place where Leone begins to believe in his own genius, and move pretentiously beyond the pure pulp brilliants of *The Good, The Bad And The Ugly*. To that, I say, "Huh? So what?" His melding of the Western epic, with its political undertones left to the storytelling, not the dialogue, combines perfectly with the refined essence of the characters and dynamic of the Western which he explored in his first three films. Ennio Morricone may produce some lavish moments of score, worthy of the Coplandesque themes of American Westerns from the 40s and 50s, but in its context it all works. To his usual triangle Leone added two tangential figures, Jill and Mr Morton - the three main characters meet these figures but don't meet each other. It works. It works brilliantly. 5/5

One Last Time:
The Post-Leone Western

It would be too much to say Leone reinvented the Western, but he certainly re-energised it. At first, many film-makers and critics dismissed him as, in Judith Crist's word, 'ersatz.' Dubbing was a sure sign of cheap foreign product, and the first reaction to the violence was repulsion. But if imitation is flattery, then Hollywood lives to flatter, and Leone's effect was soon seen everywhere. In Italy literally hundreds of Spaghetti Westerns followed, but American Westerns soon took on the look of Leone's movies, the same way ageing stars adopted the long hair and peace medallions of the young.

The films tried to imitate Leone's attitudes as well. Combined with *Bonnie And Clyde*, they tapped into the growing cynicism about the underlying 'good' values that propel the violence of the American myth. His films were the first major step forward for Westerns in a generation. Leone shifted the moral compass of the Western film; within a few years Sam Peckinpah, for example, would direct *The Wild Bunch* which, as well as its exercise in cinematic violence, is also a huge step removed from *Ride The High Country*. The Dollars films have been characterised as opening up a baroque period of indulgence with the genre. The next decade would be filled with metaphoric versions of the My Lai massacre (*Soldier Blue* (1970)), realistic, 'dirty' Westerns *(Dirty Little Billy* (1972)), Altman's deconstructive anti-Westerns (*McCabe And Mrs Miller* (1971), *Buffalo Bill And The Indians* (1976)), and Tom McGuane's extremely baroque screenplays (*Rancho Deluxe* (1975), *The Missouri Breaks* (1976)). Also, Clint Eastwood would first reprise his Leone roles and then move on to directing his own interpretations of the Western myth.

Michael Coyne dates the death of the genre in 1980, when three major Westerns, *The Long Riders, Tom Horn* and most memorably *Heaven's Gate,* flopped at the box office. Those films all seem more successful today. *The Long Riders*, by Peckinpah protégé Walter Hill, was dismissed for its gimmick of casting brothers as brothers, yet it is perhaps the truest statement of the Jesse James myth yet filmed. *Tom Horn* may be uneven, but Steve McQueen's performance is given added resonance by his subsequent death. And while *Heaven's Gate* was excoriated for its budgetary and running-time excesses (indulgences which marked the end of the 70s cult of the movie brat auteur) but its director's cut it is a magnificent work.

Heaven's Gate might better be seen as the beginning of a reversal of the Western's journey through the 60s as a super-sized personal work. The genre began to flourish once again on television, sparked by the notable 1988 mini-series *Lonesome Dove*. And Eastwood won an Oscar in 1992 for *Unforgiven,* two years after the politically-correct *Dances With Wolves* (1990) became the *Cimarron* of our time by being named Best Picture. In its wake followed black Westerns (*Posse* (1993)), Indian Westerns (*Geronimo* (1994)) and women's Westerns (*Outlaws* (1994), *Ballad Of Little Jo* (1994), *Bad Girls* (1994), *The Quick And The Dead* (1994)). Costner would play Wyatt Earp as Elliott Ness out West in *Wyatt Earp* (1994), shortly after Kurt Russell had played him more tellingly in the interesting but sometimes awkward *Tombstone* (1993), which drew heavily on Leone and Peckinpah.

It was premature to call the Western dead, or to blame its death on Leone. But Leone's next film began to suggest he might be running out of things to say about the West.

Duck, You Sucker
(aka A Fistful Of Dynamite, 1971)

Working Title: Once Upon A Time: The Revolution

Italian Title: Giu, La Testa

Italy/USA (United Artists)

Running Times: Italy 154 mins, France 150 mins, US UK 138 mins

Cast: Rod Steiger (Juan), James Coburn (Sean Mallory), Romolli Valli (Dr Villega), Domingo/Jean-Michel Antoine (Colonel Gunther Reza), Maria Monti (woman on coach), David Warbeck, Vivienne Chandler (Sean's flashbacks), Franco Graziosi (Governor), Rick Battaglia (Santerna)

Crew: Director: Sergio Leone, Producer: Fulvio Morsella, Script: Luciano Vincenzoni, Sergio Donati & Leone, Story: Leone & Donati, Photography: Giuseppe Ruzzolini, Music: Ennio Morricone, Conducted by Morricone, Editor: Nino Baragli, Art Director: Andrea Crissanti, Second Unit Directors: Giancarlo Santi & Alberto DeMartino/Martin Herbert, Second Unit Photography: Franco Delli Colli, Stunts: Benito Steffanelli

Locations: Almería, Burgos, Guadix (Spain), Dublin, Wicklow (Ireland)

Interiors: De Laurentiis Studios, Rome

Story: The Mexican Revolution 1914. Juan, a Mexican bandit, robs a luxury stagecoach along with his gang, most of whom are his sons.

They meet Sean Mallory, formerly an explosives expert with the IRA, who is dynamiting the landscape on behalf of German silver-mine speculators. Juan proposes Sean join him in robbing the bank at Mesa Verde, his lifelong dream. Sean refuses, but Juan tricks him into blowing up both the German mine owner and an army captain, making Sean an outlaw.

Sean escapes Juan by sneaking onto a passing train. Juan and his gang continue to Mesa Verde by train. On the train, Juan kills a policeman, but is saved by the intervention of Doctor Villega. In Mesa Verde, the governor's soldiers supervise executions. Sean takes Juan to a meeting of revolutionaries, who are headed by the same Dr Villega. They plan a general uprising to coincide with the attacks by Villa and Zapata on Mexico City. Their ultimate target is the bank, which Sean has arranged to be his and Juan's responsibility. They take the bank, which proves empty of money but full of political prisoners whom Juan sets free, making himself a revolutionary hero.

A Mexican army column led by Colonel Gunther Reza (in a tank) moves on Mesa Verde. Villega gives the order to disperse to caves, but Sean decides to face the column at the San Jorge Bridge. Juan stays as well, sending his niños to the grottoes to await his return. Sean and Juan stop the column and, when the soldiers seek cover under the bridge, blow it up. However, when they reach the grotto, they discover all Juan's children are dead.

The Army, led by Reza, is rounding up revolutionaries and executing them. Sean watches as Villega, who has been beaten, identifies his former compadres for Reza. In the third of four flashbacks, we see Sean's best friend, similarly beaten, identifying IRA men for the British in a pub, with Sean, waiting at the bar with a shotgun, the last to be identified.

Juan is about to be executed when Sean blows the wall he's standing against, and they escape by motorcycle. Hiding in the cattle car of a train, they observe the army massacring people in Mesa Verde and executing deserters. The governor boards the train, which is later attacked by rebels. He tries to escape through the cattle car, Juan kills him, and again is proclaimed a revolutionary hero.

On the train, Villega reappears, telling them they must buy Pancho Villa's army 24 hours by holding off Reza's units, proceeding against Villa by train. Sean, the only one who knows Villega's treachery, volunteers to ambush the train with a locomotive loaded with explosives and forces Villega to accompany him. Moving against Reza, Sean tells Villega he is not judging him, and the final flashback shows Sean in the pub killing the British soldiers and then killing his friend. As Sean jumps off the locomotive, Villega elects to go to his death as it crashes into Reza's troop train. In the ensuing battle, Reza shoots Sean three times and is killed by Juan. Getting a light from Juan, the dying Sean blows himself up in a massive explosion.

The Film With No Name: Leone's original title for the project was *Once Upon A Time: The Revolution,* and he conceived it as the second in a trilogy about the building of America. Pleasing as that is, stylistically, it doesn't fit in well between the epic scopes of *Once Upon A Time In The West* and *Once Upon A Time In America.* The title was kept for the more politically-inclined French market, but in Italy distributors feared it might be confused with Bertolucci's *Before The Revolution,* so Leone adopted the title *Giu, La Testa,* from an expression perhaps best translated from its original Italian as 'Get out of the way, dickhead.' According to Peter Bogdanovich, Leone insisted *Duck, You Sucker,* the simpler translation into American, was an everyday phrase in the US, but it jars whenever Coburn, in his brogue, uses it. The film was called *A Fistful Of Dynamite* in the UK, which is a more commercial title, and when the US release flopped, the UK title was adopted hastily. It is most often available these days under that title, which is a perfectly good one, but we've kept to the one closest to the Italian original. Personally, I prefer the *Once Upon A Time* version, although stylistically the film simply does not fit with the other two of the purported trilogy.

A Fistful Of Motifs: The religious motifs abound, starting with the spoiled priest in the luxury carriage of the opening scene. When Juan takes the aristocratic woman off into the bushes, as it were, and places her hand on his organ, she says "Oh Jesus," (pause) "Help me. I'm going to faint." (To which Juan replies, "if you faint you'll miss the best part.") When Juan meets Sean organ music rises and he sees Sean like an angel in a Mexican shrine, with the Bank of Mesa Verde his shrine. Similar music will greet the Bank itself. Before blowing up Juan's coach, Sean prays at its altar. Sean's nitroglycerine is called 'holy water' throughout. When Juan discovers his children killed, he tears the cross from around his neck, just before Sean dies he gives it back to Juan, as if restoring his faith through dying. Juan's last words, "what will I do now?" recall the disciples after the death of Christ.

Duck, You Sucker is perhaps Leone's most self-referential film, particularly in the gradual revelation of Sean's flashbacks, which echo Mortimer's in *For A Few Dollars More* and Harmonica's in *Once Upon A Time In The West*. These are not triggered by a musical source within the action, but by Morricone's 'Sean, Sean, Sean' theme.

Juan's obsession with The Bank of Mesa Verde recalls Indio's with the Bank of El Paso. Dr Villega's opening scene on the train, where he holds a book in front of his face, recalls Colonel Mortimer's introduction in *For A Few Dollars More*. The caves where the rebels hide recall *Collossus Of Rhodes,* and just as Leone used the Colossus as a prison for rebels, so too the Bank of Mesa Verde, whatever it symbolises to Juan, is actually being used as a political prison.

It's hard to avoid the idea that by this point Leone was aware of his influence on Sam Peckinpah, and that this film, with its Mexican setting, highlights some of their differences in approach to the same violent material. The opening titles, over silence, quote Mao on the violence of revolution (while omitting the final line, 'by which one class overthrows another'). At the same time Peckinpah was opening *Straw Dogs* (1971) with a quotation from Lao Tze. In a scene cut from the US/UK version, the opening credits were followed by a scene of Juan pissing on ants crawling up a tree, recalling the opening of *The Wild Bunch*, where children use ants to torment a scorpion. Peeing is an important motif in both *The Good, The Bad And The Ugly* (where Tuco escapes from Wallace while peeing) and in *Once Upon A Time In America* (whilst spying on Deborah, Noodles is interrupted by a man using the loo; Noodles encounters Peggy needing to pee in the communal toilet; the boys set fire to a news-stand using kerosene squirted in imitation of peeing).

The Wild Bunch also played on the presence of Germans in its Mexican revolution setting. Here we never see any, but Sean is employed by German mining interests and the Mexican Colonel Reza is presented as a German panzer commander (the actor, Domingo Antoine, looks remarkably like the young James Woods). But Juan's machine-gun scenes are more reminiscent of Richard Brooks' *The Professionals* (1966), another film which seems to have figured in Leone's imagination. It starred Robert Ryan, Woody Strode, James Coburn and Lee Marvin, all of whom Leone either cast or considered, as well as Claudia Cardinale as the kidnapped wife the Professionals are hired to retrieve. Jack Palance, about to begin his own Spaghetti Western career, played the bandit with whom she wishes to stay.

Leone's political view was an interesting variant on the typical revolutionary pattern followed by other Spaghetti Western directors, who often aimed to be more directly political. In fact, Luciano Vincenzoni worked on the script of Corbucci's *A Professional Gun* (1968) which had a Polish mercenary teaming up with a Mexican miner-turned-revolutionary, and featured an airplane attack on the rebels. "The Polack." as he is called, does not care which side he is on, as long as he gets paid, while the Mexican, originally satisfied with banditry, becomes more and more committed to the revolution. (Jack Palance features as well, as a homosexual gunman called Curly, who crosses himself after killing.)

In *Duck, You Sucker*, Coburn enters the film blowing up the Mexican landscape on behalf of German mining interests, yet it is he, bitter as he is over the failures of the IRA against the British, who hooks up with the revolutionaries and entices Juan to unwittingly join him. He does this even though his motto, 'duck, you sucker,' in its Italian origins would imply 'don't take sides,' and 'stay out of the way' (much as Joe had done to his profit in *A Fistful Of Dollars*). We can also surmise that Sean has become an anarchist (he is reading Bakunin in one scene) and may enjoy the chaos of the Mexican revolution. Although Juan repeatedly makes himself a hero, he is still not committed to the revolution when Coburn blows himself up.

Leone's aim (and perhaps that of writers Vincenzoni and Sergio Donati) was to satirise the demand for political films, the insistence of many critics that the cinema must carry messages, and that cinema was the ideal medium to carry them in direct, dialectical fashion. Looking at the experience of Leone's father, whose socialist beliefs may have cost him part of his career, the relative lack of impact Leftist politics had on Italy during the post-war era, and also given the frustratingly temporary nature of any effects of the revolution in Mexico, it is no surprise that Leone should take a somewhat cynical approach to the revolutionary nature of films about the Mexican revolution! Yet French critics in particular praised *Duck, You Sucker* for its political content and, in contrast to its failure in the US, was his most successful film in France up to that time.

Duck Soup: It is true that, following the success of *Once Upon A Time In The West,* Leone wanted to be taken more seriously as a film-maker. He had 'signed' a short documentary film, *The Twelfth Of December* (1971), along with 11 other Italian film-makers, including Visconti, Zavattini and Brass. The film dealt with the news coverage and official line concerning the terrorist bombing of the Banca dell'Agricoltura in Milan and the death of the accused bomber, Giuseppe Pinelli. Pinelli's death, in a 'fall' from the police station, would lead to the film *Investigation Of A Citizen Above Suspicion* (Elio Petri, 1969) and more directly, to Dario Fo's play *The Accidental Death Of An Anarchist* (1970). Leone's switch to a more overtly political subject and the choice of the Bank of Mesa Verde (green plains/ farmers) would seem to be a carry-over from the Milan bombing.

It was around this point that Paramount offered Leone the Mario Puzo novel, *The Godfather*, to direct. But he had already conceived his own gangster film, *Once Upon A Time In America,* as part of his Once Upon A Time trilogy, and for whatever reason (there would be a variety of stories) he turned it down.

It is also true that Leone had grown tired of the grind of directing, and was finding it harder and harder emotionally to actually finish a film, and submit it to the world. So while he bandied about extravagant projects like a remake of *Gone With The Wind*, he had set up a production company, Rafran, in partnership with Claudio Mancini and his brother-in-law Fulvio Morsella. He appeared to want to move into the kind of creative producer role which had been rare in Hollywood before the days of High Concept, but which had been defined by some of the greats of the industry, from Val Lewton on a small scale to David O Selznick on a somewhat grander one.

So from the start, Leone considered various American directors to helm *Duck, You Sucker,* starting with Peter Bogdanovich, who might seem an unlikely choice today, but at the time had been best known as a John Ford scholar, whose first feature was the promising *Targets* (1968). He had not yet achieved his breakthrough with the remarkable second feature, *The Last Picture Show* (1971). Bogdanovich and Leone failed to see eye-to-eye (the reworking in the flashback sequences of Irish motifs from Ford's *The Informer* and *The Quiet Man* couldn't have pleased Bogdanovich). Leone also approached Sam Peckinpah, and the two met to discuss the project, but never agreed to work together. The mind boggles at how that relationship would have proceeded, given Leone's reactions to American excess on the films he worked on in the 1950s, and Peckinpah's characteristic bristling at any form of creative control. Eventually, Giancarlo Santi, the assistant director on *The Good, The Bad And The Ugly* and *Once Upon A Time In The West,* began the project as director, but Leone, who was controlling everything anyway, quickly took the reins again, especially since Rod Steiger demanded to be directed by Leone and no one else.

Steiger's role had been offered to Eli Wallach; the Coburn role to Jason Robards, Malcolm MacDowell and even Eastwood. Wallach was not considered a big enough box-office draw by the American producers. Coburn had been Leone's second choice (after Henry Fonda) for the Man With No Name.

High Art: Leone was an avid collector of art and often used specific artists to set the tone of his films. While filming in Spain he haunted Madrid's Prado, where he and Tonino Delli Colli found much of the inspiration in the shooting of *For A Few Dollars More* from Goya. It's easy to see images from El Greco as well, in the long dark faces and bodies with which Leone litters his background gangs. Leone loved the dark Goya, and traces of other painters who use darkness and lighting effects within it, like Rembrandt, can also be seen in all his later films. In a recent interview, Eli Wallach recalled Leone's obsession with Vermeer. Tuco with his pink parasol, following Blondie's horse through the desert, recalls DiChirico and other surrealists; the two could even be the angular Don Quixote and Sancho Panza, another tale dear to Leone's heart. There are also specific references in *Once Upon A Time In America* to both Degas, in the dance sequence, and to Reginald Marsh, in the Coney Island billboard which combines a couple of his paintings, and then dissolves to a Peter Max big apple in 1968.

Just as Ford reconstructed specific Remington effects and paintings in *She Wore A Yellow Ribbon* (1949) and *Fort Apache*, Leone and Ruzzolini brilliantly reconstructed Goya's 'The Third Of May In Madrid: The Executions On Principe Pio Hill,' in *Duck, You Sucker's* most poignant scene, as Sean watches Villega point out rebels to Reza for execution. Villega has been tortured and does this to save himself from more pain. In an echo of *The Good, The Bad And The Ugly,* the whole scene is filmed in the rain, lighted by the car headlights, an effect which would be reprised in the scenes of Noodles looking at the bodies of his friends in *Once Upon A Time In America.*

Verdict: This is by far the weakest of Leone's mature works, yet upon re-viewing it seems to improve. A major problem with the English version is that this is one of the ultimate bad-accent movies: Coburn's

Oirish brogue is bad enough but Steiger's Mexican is a strain on the credibility and the ears throughout: There are even times when the two actors' accents appear to meld into one!

The ultimate tension in the film seems dissipated between the two main characters and a shifting third. The classic Leone triangle could be constructed either with Dr Villega as the Colonel Mortimer or with Colonel Reza as Angel Eyes, but as it stands neither character is able to break into the dynamic between the two leads.

Steiger wouldn't necessarily allow that. Where Eli Wallach's scene-stealing seems almost natural and his ratlike playing remains consistent, one often gets the sense Steiger is seeing what he can get away with, and Coburn sometimes seems simply resigned to watching. Not surprisingly, Steiger's best scenes come when his range is most proscribed: in the early 'rape' of the woman in the carriage, where Maria Monti's reactions take the lead, or in his final scene, where he must react to Coburn's underplayed sentimentality.

Leone also appears to miss his stock company. Although there are scenes of individual brilliance, particularly the execution in the rain and the massive set piece at the bridge, the overall look lacks the sustained brilliance which his long-term collaborators Tonino Delli Colli and Carlo Simi might have brought to it.

Similarly, Mickey Knox's claims to have played a bigger creative role (beyond just literal translation) in the final script of *The Good, The Bad And The Ugly* and *Once Upon A Time In The West* are given some credence by the relative flatness and absence of humour in the English dialogue of *Duck, You Sucker* (a function which Stuart Kaminsky would provide in *Once Upon A Time In America*). The lines that should be memorable, of which there are so many in *The Good, The Bad And The Ugly* and *Once Upon A Time In The West,* here lack that sharpness of English which worked so well for Eastwood, Wallach, Van Cleef, Robards, Fonda and Bronson. 3/5

The Long Intermezzo

After *Duck, You Sucker* Leone's determination to relax from the pressures of directing seemed finally to win out. But his next project was to produce, for Rafran, *My Name Is Nobody* (1973), which would be directed by his long-time assistant Tonino Valerii. Valerii already had six credits as a director, coincidentally the same number as his mentor, so he wasn't exactly inexperienced. Four of his films were Westerns, including the hugely successful *Day Of Anger* (1967) with Lee Van Cleef.

Although many commentators like to see Leone as the puppet master, using a director he could manipulate, any viewing of the film should disabuse them of that notion. Although there are many Leone touches, and many pieces of direct commentary either on, or evidently by, Leone, the film moves away from Leone's style to concentrate on a more straightforward and comic presentation.

Leone contributed the original idea, or maybe it was Sergio Donati, depending on whose story one believes, but it began with the concept of recreating the Odyssey in the West and soon evolved into a comment on Enzo Barboni's comic Westerns starring Terence Hill as Trinity, which had actually outperformed Leone's at the box office.

Leone might have started out with the idea of being a 'creative' producer, and controlling the director, but the film is very much Valerii's. According to De Fornari's interview with Valerii, Leone's vision of satirising the almost slapstick *Trinity* was that Hill's Nobody would play straight man to Henry Fonda's Jack Beauregard, so that the artificial clown would be outshone by the real Western gunman, and in effect the Trinity character would be killed off. However, to get Hill to play Nobody, more sympathetic comic scenes were added to the screenplay, and Leone had trouble finding a director. So when Valerii agreed to direct the film, he insisted the story be about Hill's hero-worship of the older gunfighter, and Leone agreed. Valerii did all the shooting in America himself, and only when the production fell behind schedule in Spain and Henry Fonda's availability was slipping away, did Leone direct some second-unit sequences with Hill, including the duel of the glasses parodied in *Tombstone*.

Producer Claudio Mancini warned Valerii that once Leone did any work on the film people would say he directed the picture, and Valerii

72

himself notes wryly that Steven Spielberg called *My Name Is Nobody* Leone's best film.

Leone would also get in his digs at Sam Peckinpah, whose name is shown on a tombstone in a graveyard, with Nobody unable to pronounce it. There are also slow-motion scenes which echo Peckinpah. Fonda seems dressed and equipped with glasses which echo Joel McCrea's in *Ride The High Country,* and there is a final shoot-out which matches up Fonda's Beauregard against the Wild Bunch - in this case a 'gang' of some 150 gunmen, who ride down on the lone Fonda while Wagner plays on the soundtrack. This was all well before *Apocalypse Now* (1979), and there were almost four times as many guns as Fuller's 40! Certainly those critics who saw Leone's baroque Westerns as hailing the end of the genre would be convinced that there was nowhere to go from here.

But there was. In 1977 Leone produced *Un Genio, Due Comparii, Un Pollo* (literally, 'a genius, two buddies, an idiot,' the title playing on *The Good, The Bad And The Ugly),* better known in English as *Nobody Is The Greatest*. This one makes *My Name Is Nobody* look like *Ride Lonesome*. Hill reprises his Trinity/Nobody character (here called Joe Thanks) alongside the French-Canadian singing star Robert Charlebois and the wonderful French actress Miou-Miou, who appears to be wondering what she's doing there! Leone would produce five other features for Rafran in this period, including *Il Gatto* (*The Cat*, 1977) a light-hearted police comedy directed by Luigi Comencini. He had come full circle since assisting Comencini in 1952. *Il Giocattolo* (*The Toy*, 1978) was a thriller, directed by Giuliano Montaldo from a screenplay by Sergio Donati. The other three were comedies, directed by and starring the comic Carlo Verdone: *Un Sacco Bello* (*Fun Is Beautiful*, 1979), *Bianco, Rosso E Verdone* (*Red, White And 'Green,'* 1981) and *Troppo Forte* (*He's Too Much*, 1985). In the last one, Leone actually directed one scene, a motorcycle chase around Rome. During this time, he also made another acting appearance, playing himself at the Cannes Film Festival in Michael Ritchie's *An Almost Perfect Affair* (1979).

Nowadays it is commonplace for directors to move from commercials to feature films, but during this time Leone made the move the other way. In 1974 he began directing commercials and would continue making them until the end of his life. It helped pay the bills, certainly, but it may have also been a way of exercising his visual imagination without the creative pressure and hassles feature films had brought to him. However, he would accept the pressures once again for what would be, sadly, his final feature. It was the culmination of almost twenty years of interest and work on a project that began with a gangster novel called *The Hoods*.

Once Upon A Time In America (1984)

USA (Ladd Company/Warner Brothers)

Running Times: Italy 238 mins, UK 228 mins, USA 159 mins (restored 226 mins)

Cast: Robert De Niro (Noodles), James Woods (Max), Elizabeth McGovern (Deborah), William Forsythe (Cockeye), James Hayden (Patsy), Tuesday Weld (Carol), Darlanne Fluegel (Eve), Treat Williams (Jimmy O'Donnell), Joe Pesci (Frankie Menaldi), Burt Young (Joe From Detroit), Danny Aiello (Chief Aiello), Larry Rapp (Fat Moe), Amy Ryder (Peggy), Dutch Miller (Van Linden), Robert Harper (Sharkey), Richard Bright (Chicken Joe), Gerard Murphy (Crowning), Mario Brega (Mandy), Olga Karlatos (Woman In Puppet Theatre), Ray Dittrich (Trigger), Frank Gio (Beely), Karen Shallo (Mrs Aiello), Angelo Florio (Willie The Ape), Scott Tiler (Young Noodles), Jennifer Connelly (Young Deborah), Rusty Jacobs (Young Max/David), Brian Bloom (Young Patsy), Adrian Curran (Young Cockeye), Mike Monetti (Young Moe), Julie Cohen (Young Peggy), Noah Moazezi (Dominic), James Russo (Bugsy), Frankie Caserta, Joey Marzella (Bugsy's Gang), Clem Caserta (Al Capuano), Frank Sisto (Fred Capuano), Jerry Strivelli (Johnny Capuano), Ann Neville (Girl In Coffin), Mike Gendel (Irving Gold), Marvin Scott (TV Interviewer), Paul Herman (Monkey), Joey Faye (Adorable Old Man), Linda Ipanema (Nurse Thompson), Tandy Cronin (1st Reporter), Richard Zobel (2nd Reporter), Baxter Harris (3rd Reporter), Arnon Milchan (Chauffeur), Bruno Iannone (Thug), Marty Licata (Cemetery Caretaker), Marcia Jean Kurtz (Moe's Mother), Estelle Harris (Peggy's Mother), Richard Foronji (Whitey), Gerritt Debeer (Drunk), Alexander Godfrey (Newsie), Cliff Cudney (Mounted Policeman), Bruce Bahrenburg (Sgt Halloran), Mort Freeman (Street Singer), Sandra Solberg (Friend Of Young Deborah), Jay Zeeley (Foreman), Massimo Liti (Young Cacro)

Uncredited: Claudio Mancini (O'Donnell's Assitant)

Crew: Director: Sergio Leone, Producer: Arnon Milchan, Executive Producer: Claudio Mancini, Script: Leonardo Benvenuti, Piero De Bernardi, Enrico Medioli, Franco Arcalli, Franco Ferrini & Leone, Additional Dialogue: Stuart Keminsky, Based on the novel *The Hoods*, by Harry Grey, Photography: Tonino Delli Colli Music: Ennio Morricone, conducted by Morricone, Art Director: Carlo Simi, Editor: Nino Barágli, Sound: Jean-Pierre Ruhu, Stunts: Benito Steffanelli, Musicians: Edda Dell'Orso (vocals), Gheorghe Zamfir (Pan pipes)

Locations: New York, Hoboken, St Petersburg (Florida), Montreal, Trois Rivières, Paris, Venice, Bellagio, Pietralata

Interiors: Cinecittà, Rome

Story: New York, December 3, 1933, following the repeal of Prohibition. Four gangsters searching for Noodles murder his girlfriend

Eve and torture his friend Fat Moe. Noodles lies in an opium den, distraught over the deaths of his three friends Max, Cockeye and Patsy in a police ambush. Noodles hears the sound of a phone ringing. While the phone rings we see scenes of his friends' bodies, of the celebrations of the ending of prohibition and a phone ringing on a policeman's desk. Noodles' reverie is interrupted by the arrival of the hoods searching for him. He escapes, returns to Moe's, kills the hood left to keep watch for him and picks up a key hidden in a grandfather clock. He takes the key to the bus station and retrieves a suitcase, expecting to find a million dollars, but finds it stuffed with the same newspaper he read in the opium den. He buys a one-way ticket on the first bus leaving, to Buffalo. He exits through a gate.

1968: Noodles returns to New York through the same gate. He finds Fat Moe and tells him he has received an anonymous note telling him to visit the graves of his former partners.

1922: Noodles and his three friends Patsy, Cockeye and Dominic grow up in the Jewish ghetto of the Lower East Side (though Dominic is presumably Italian). Their circle includes Moe's sister Deborah, who dreams of being an actress and whom Noodles worships from afar, and Peggy, who already trades sexual favours for her favourite pastries. Into this group comes Max - when Noodles' gang were stopped from rolling a drunk by Whitey aka 'Fart-Face,' the local cop, Max manages to snatch the drunk's expensive pocket watch. Whitey is on the take from the boys' other nemesis, Bugsy, the local small-time hood. Max and Noodles become friends. The boys catch Whitey having sex with Peggy and blackmail him. Noodles has his first, short-lived, sexual experience with Peggy and stands by while Max, after having trouble getting an erection, is more successful with her. While her family are at Sabbath, Deborah brings Noodles to watch her dance. She recites verses from the 'Song Of Songs' to him, adding ironic comments about his shortcomings, saying "he's altogether loveable, but he'll always be a two-bit punk, so he'll never be my beloved. What a shame." As they kiss, they realise someone is watching through the peephole; it is Max who calls Noodles away. They are beaten by Bugsy's gang; Deborah hides behind the door as the bloody Noodles begs for her to let him in.

Noodles sells the Capuano brothers a foolproof method of saving bootleg booze jettisoned from boats during police chase. When the boys retrieve the crates that have bobbed up to the surface, Noodles and Max fall in the water, and Max pretends to have drowned. The five boys agree to pool half their earnings and store it in a suitcase in the bus-station locker, leaving the key with Fat Moe. Bugsy encounters the gang and shoots Dominic. Noodles kills Bugsy, but also knives a cop and is sent to jail.

1968: In the mausoleum where his friends are buried, Noodles finds a plaque saying the mausoleum itself has been built by him. Hanging on the plaque is a locker key. In the locker Noodles finds a suitcase full of money, 'an advance on your next job.' Carrying the suitcase, in the 'modern' New York, a nervous Noodles ducks an arm catching a Frisbee, which cuts to…

1932: Max grabbing Noodles' suitcase on his release from prison, where the gang have met him with a hearse, part of their legit cover as funeral operators. The young woman's corpse in the coffin is actually a naked whore procured to welcome Noodles back. Behind the family restaurant, Fat Moe's is now a successful speakeasy, Peggy is a thriving madam, while Deborah now dances at the Palace Theatre. As Noodles talks seriously with Deborah, Max, looking on jealously, again calls him away. They meet with big-time gangster Frankie Menaldi, who wants them to rob a jeweller in Detroit for his friend Joe. The job has been set up by the jeweller's nymphomaniac secretary, Carol. During the robbery, Carol asks Noodles to hit her to make it look real. She is so demanding Noodles tosses her on a desk and rapes her, to her evident pleasure.

After getting the pay-off from Joe, the gang, without Noodles' foreknowledge, double-cross Joe and kill him. Noodles chases Joe's last henchman into a chicken plant and kills him. Max explains Menaldi wanted Joe dead, but he knew Noodles wouldn't agree to the double-cross. Noodles argues against going into business with Menaldi, asking what Max would do when Menaldi eventually asks one of them to kill the other. When Max suggests they go for a swim Noodles drives the car into the lake.

1968: On the TV news at Fat Moe's, we see a blown-up car containing the remains of District Attorney Lister, the second figure to have died in the scandals surrounding Secretary Bailey. The charges of corruption facing Bailey involve union boss Jimmy O'Donnell, whom we see interviewed, and who Noodles knows…

1932: Idealistic young union organiser O'Donnell is about to be burned to death by Chicken Joe when the gang turn up with factory owner Crowning and exchange prisoners. O'Donnell at first resists their help, but after the police bust the strike and escort scabs into the factory, the gang switch the babies around in a maternity ward and blackmail corrupt Police Chief Aiello with the threat of never finding his newborn son.

Carol now commutes to New York on weekends, working in Peggy's whorehouse while her husband watches. She fails to recognise the gang, who don masks and ask her to recognise the one who fucked her during the robbery. She chooses Max.

Noodles takes Deborah to a lavish romantic evening, where she again explains that although she'd 'probably even enjoy' being kept under lock and key by Noodles, she has to have her own life. When Noodles recites from 'Song Of Songs' she tells him she is leaving for Hollywood the next day. In the car going back, Noodles rapes her. The next day, he stands on the platform, still in last night's tuxedo, watching her train leave; when she sees him she pulls down the curtain in her compartment.

Noodles returns to the gang after a period away, where he had been "at the Chinks" lost in opium dreams, and so out of it he called Cockeye "Deborah" when the gang tracked him down. In the meantime, the union has paid off the gang and Max has acquired both a throne and a moll (Carol). Jimmy O'Donnell, while calling the gang for more help, is wounded in an ambush. The gang retaliate by killing Chicken Joe and his sidekick as they get their pay-off from Crowning, while leaving Crowning standing unharmed outside his club. In O'Donnell's hospital room, corrupt politician Sharkey suggests the gang should get into the union and other legit businesses, as Prohibition will not last forever. Noodles walks out, saying he doesn't trust politicians and is going to the beach. Max chases him, they leave for Florida as Frankie Menaldi heads up to the hospital room.

1933: On holiday in Miami, Max (with Carol) and Noodles (with new girlfriend Eve) learn of the imminent repeal of Prohibition. Max wants to go out with a bang, robbing the Federal Reserve Bank in New York. When Noodles calls him crazy, Max, in a rage, punches him. Back in New York, Carol asks Noodles to do something to prevent the sure failure of the robbery. Fat Moe stages a Funeral for Prohibition, which we saw in Noodles' opening dream; he leaves the party to make the phone call to police Sgt Halloran, to have the gang arrested as they make a final pick-up of bootleg booze. This will give them short jail sentences, and avoid Max's robbery scheme. Max tells Noodles he's losing his nerve, and when Noodles again calls him crazy Max again goes into a rage and clubs him unconscious.

1968: Noodles tracks down Carol at the Bailey Foundation. She tells him Max had set up the whole scheme of betrayal, intending his own death because he feared he would die crazy like his father. Noodles discovers that Deborah is the 'patron saint' of the Foundation. He visits Deborah backstage after she performs as Cleopatra. Noodles, who has learned from Carol that Deborah and Bailey are lovers, wants to know why he has been invited to a party at Bailey's Long Island mansion. Apparently unchanged by time, Deborah tells Noodles to leave New York. A young man calls for her. When Noodles leaves, he chooses not to take the side door Deborah has suggested, and meets David, who is Bailey's son, and the image of the young Max (David is Noodles' name). At Bailey's party, Max tells Noodles he ran off with the money and eventually got Deborah as well. Now facing ruin over the corruption scandal, he wants Noodles to kill him. Noodles refuses to admit that Bailey is Max and says the killing is the kind of job his gang would never touch. He leaves. Walking away from the mansion, he sees the figure of Max follow him. When a garbage truck passes that figure, compactor churning, the figure has disappeared. The truck's rear lights become the lights of a 1933 car whose occupants are celebrating the end of Prohibition, but driving past the mansion in 1968. In 1933, Noodles enters the opium den. He sucks at the pipe, then lies back and as the camera moves overhead, through a gauzy canopy we watch as his face finally opens into a broad, childlike, smile.

Grey Areas: As befits a film some 15 years in the making *Once Upon A Time In America* is certainly Leone's most ambitious work, and in some ways his most controversial. He had first encountered the story when his brother-in-law, Fulvio Morsella, read him Harry Grey's novel. Grey (né Goldberg) was a former inmate of Sing-Sing who was writing first-hand about his experiences, from childhood onward, but what appealed to Leone was the way its scenes were so obviously drawn from the great early gangster movies. He met Grey in 1968, and began the long process of trying to get the film rights, which had been bought by Joseph E Levine and sold on to John Ford actor-turned-producer Dan Curtis. An original treatment was done by Ernesto Gastaldi.

Leone would later accuse American writer Robert Dillon of having stolen his opening to use on John Frankenheimer's *99 44/100% Dead* (1974). In this, the crash of a car into the Hudson River turns into a pan of the cars and dead bodies at the river bottom. Leone's pan, from a weighted body, would show a veritable cemetery, then rise above the water to pan the Statue of Liberty, over which the film's title would appear!

Producer Alberto Grimaldi secured the rights, but wanted an American screenwriter. Pete Hammill, whose screenplay for *Doc* had turned Wyatt Earp's Tombstone into Tammany Hall, was approached to write the screenplay, but after he turned them down, they hired Norman Mailer, another close friend of Mickey Knox. Mailer worked three weeks non-stop in a Rome hotel room and took the script with him to the Thrilla in Manila, but apparently produced nothing usable, apart perhaps from a convoluted flashback sequence with a certain Proustian feel. In fact, Noodles quotes Proust directly, but his lines almost certainly post-date Mailer's participation.

Leone worked with two of Italy's top writers, Enrico Medioli and Franco Arcalli, to produce a workable draft. Medioli, who worked with Visconti on *The Leopard, Rocco And His Brothers* (1960) and *The Damned* (1969), and would wind up concentrating on the 1930s prohibition era. Medioli noticed how precise Leone wanted the script to be, because he knew he would drag out tempos while shooting and editing. Arcalli, who was also a film editor and had worked with Bertolucci on *The Conformist* (1971) and *Last Tango In Paris* (1973), was particularly valuable in seeing the visual transitions so crucial to the flashback structure. Leone once again gave a critic a start, this time Franco Ferrari was brought in and would research the childhood scenes from 1922. When the shooting script was complete, it ran some 317 pages.

Crime novelist Stuart Kaminsky, who had also written works of criticism on Leone and Clint Eastwood, was brought in. He refined the dialogue and sharpened the characters of the gang, especially Max and Noodles. It was Kaminsky who insisted that Noodles' revelation to Deborah that he read the 'Song Of Songs' each night in prison did not include the fact he also masturbated to it!

Heroes Within Society: For the first time since *Colossus Of Rhodes,* Leone sites his heroes within the workings of society, and the only 'duel' within the film is a battle of wills and memory in the final scene between James Woods and Robert De Niro.

Leone was offered *The Godfather* as a project soon after Paramount acquired the rights, but turned it down. The reasons he gave at the time involved not wanting to work in his own 'native' mythology, that of the Sicilian Mafia. From Paramount's point of view, the very fact that he was Italian was probably a major factor in offering him the job, as he would be immune from accusations of anti-Italian stereotyping. So it is significant that the gangsters in *Once Upon A Time In America* are specifically Jewish, which allows Leone his 'outsider' perspective, and that their gang falls apart as it is assimilated both into the larger scale workings of both the Mafia and specifically American politics. It is possible to look at *Once Upon A Time In America* as *The Godfather, Parts I* and *II* together in one movie, with the Lower East Side replacing Sicily. In that sense, Jewish gangsters learned their trade in the new world, while Italian gangsters had brought theirs with them from Sicily. Yet his star, Robert De Niro, without whose participation the project would never have taken off, is Italian and had done youthful gangster roles in both *Mean Streets* (1973) and *Godfather II* (1974). Among the actors considered were Gérard Depardieu and Richard Dreyfuss (with Jean Gabin and James Cagney as the elderly Noodles and Max), or the team of Tom Berenger and Paul Newman.

An American Dream: In approaching his biggest work, his first American work and his first work placed firmly inside society, Leone adopted his most complex and challenging storytelling format, involving a series of audacious jumps in time which reflect a level of ambiguity. As a result, the success of the film depends primarily on how the audience reacts to ambiguity, and how far they are willing to suspend their disbelief and enter into Leone's, and perhaps Noodles', fairy tale. Even if you prefer, like the Ladd Company, to see the story as being literally 'true', you still are left with the question of Max's fate. Has he been gobbled up by the garbage truck, or has he, as he did in his opening scene, used it to make a getaway?

Whichever way you interpret that, there are at least two problems with accepting the story literally. The first is Max's rise in politics, which seems unlikely given his relatively high profile as a gangster (surely there was somebody who would recognise him, who couldn't be, as Carol presumably was, kept silent by bribe or intimidation?) The other is the apparent non-ageing of Deborah, who, when she strips her kabuki make-up off in 1968, appears virtually the same as when her train left for Hollywood in 1933 (and this was in the era before massive cosmetic surgery, à la Cher or Jane Fonda was commonplace). It doesn't help that Elisabeth McGovern's face is particularly free from angles, edges or lines (one critic once described her as looking like the world's most beautiful painted balloon). With the Cleopatra reference, Leone has set us up for a timeless woman, but still, it requires some accepting.

It is easy to see this as a fairy tale, in which terms Leone was fond of describing his films, and thus suspend our disbelief to accept Max's new identity and Deborah's eternal youth, just as we may have already suspended it to accept the young characters, both in their seeming age differences from each other, and also in their substantial changes when they hit adulthood. How, for example, has the young baby Buddha-shaped Fat Moe morphed into the figure who runs the speakeasy? In such a context, Deborah as Noodles' ageless love makes dramatic, if not celebrity film magazine, sense.

Or we can read, as Stuart Kaminsky first suggested, the entire film as Noodles' extended opium dream, which starts with the shattering noise which announces the arrival of the thugs searching for him. Seen in this way, with the dream beginning with Noodles' escape from the opium den, the entire film becomes Noodles' own way of justifying his betrayal of his friends, an elaborate fantasy which makes Max the villain, makes his (and Deborah's) life successful in business (or artistic) terms, but empty in human terms, and thus leaves Noodles with the moral high ground.

Once Upon Two Or Three Times: Leone was contracted to deliver a film of 165 minutes to the Ladd Company, but his 'final' cut was 229 minutes. The trail of long movies that had bombed at the box office (Bertolucci's *1900* (1977), *Heaven's Gate*, *The Right Stuff* (1983)) and the responses of a sneak-preview audience in Boston to Leone's version convinced Ladd to cut the film. This despite a successful showing at Cannes in May 1984.

Editor Zach Staenburg dropped the time-cut structure and put together a version which ran 144 minutes and followed a straightforward time sequence, starting with young Noodles spying on Deborah dancing in 1922 and ending with a dubbed gunshot which made it clear Bailey had committed suicide. Deborah disappeared on the train to Hollywood. When this version opened in America, it received almost universally dismissive reviews.

There was one exception. Mary Corliss' review in *Film Comment* had a brilliant commentary on the effect of the telephone rings in De Niro's opening sequence: 'it's easy to imagine that after about five rings, Alan Ladd Jr was trying to determine what Leone was up to; that after ten he decided it was to inflict pain on the audience; that after fifteen he envisioned members of the audience shouting out "answer the bloody phone!"; that after twenty rings he wished he was (sic) in some other business; and that on the twenty-second ring he resolved to cut the damn movie down to a running time that exhibitors would find acceptable.' But Corliss seemed to share Ladd's consternation. She is almost unique in preferring, perversely, the cut version to the original, finding it 'reshaped Leone's mesmerising, intermittently powerful botch of a movie into a 145-minute film that is within shooting distance of a masterpiece.'

Leone's original 228-minute cut, with two minutes trimmed to qualify for an R rating, was finally released in the USA following a successful re-preview at the New York Film Festival, prompting an immediate critical re-evaluation. There is also a version cut for NBC television, in the USA, of approximately 190 minutes, shown in two 120-minute time slots (allowing for commercials). Many sources refer to a version of 265 minutes, done for Italian TV, which contains scenes to which there is no equivalent in the US/UK versions. According to Frayling, the scenes referred to exist, but have never been dubbed, and no such version has ever been shown.

For A Few Scenes More: In the final cuts, the character who suffered most was Darlanne Fleugel as Eve. If you look closely, you may spot her in an elevator following the scene in Jimmy O'Donnell's hospital room. In the film as is, Eve makes her first appearance in Miami as Noodles' girl. But as originally shot, she is a hooker who picks up Noodles as he drinks to drown his sorrows following Deborah's departure for Hollywood. He gives her $1,000 as long as he can call her "Deborah" then passes out in bed reciting the 'Song Of Songs,' which young Deborah had once recited to him to show her love. Then Noodles bumps into her in the elevator, she again takes him to bed and this time reveals her falsies to him. A still of Fleugel in bed with her breasts exposed is included in De Fornari's book, and this is an important scene because it is the only time (at least since Peggy went to the loo in front of him) that anyone will expose their true self to Noodles, and it contrasts with Deborah's elaborate make-up removal in her Cleopatra scene.

The next morning, Max breaks in on them and says "let's go to the beach", meaning Miami; the production still from this scene shows up

82

frequently; it was used in the NFT's programme booklet when they ran their season of Leone films in April 2000. In the film as is, Max says "let's go to the beach" in the hospital lobby, having caught up with De Niro on the other elevator. Significantly, in that scene, the two pass by Joe Pesci as Frank Menardi, who is heading for O'Donnell's room which implies that Max, via Sharkey, is actually dealing with Menardi again. This recalls Noodles asking Max what he would do when Menardi inevitably suggested one turn on the other, a question Max never actually answered at the time.

With Fleugel's scenes lost, there is no establishing Eve's character when she shows up in Miami; we recognise her as the woman murdered in the opening scene of the film, but have no idea of how she came to be at Noodles' side. And there is really no set-up for her final scene, where she shows real loss when Noodles tells her he may not see her for some time, because he may be going to jail with the gang. Fleugel, a former model whose best role before *Once Upon A Time In America* was in *Battle Beyond The Stars* (a 1980 SF version of *The Magnificent Seven*, scripted by John Sayles), never made the breakthrough to stardom, which perhaps might have been helped by her lost scenes.

Louise Fletcher, an Oscar winner in *One Flew Over The Cuckoos Nest* (1975), played the director of the cemetery, but her role, which consisted mostly of explaining the Egyptian Book of the Dead to Noodles, was cut completely. Jimmy O'Donnell's part shrunk as well: some of the explanatory material about his union's struggles with management thugs and the police was lost (see *F.I.S.T.* (1978) or *Hoffa* (1992) if you need to be filled in) as well as a final scene with Bailey in which Treat Williams tells James Woods that suicide is his only way out. In this scene their roles are reversed from earlier in the film, where O'Donnell is the politically naïve one, and Woods the astute one who points out the former's mistakes.

The Dead Shall Live: The film opens with Eve coming home to find a bullet-hole outline of Noodles' body in their bed and the hoods waiting for her smash his picture. He is, in a sense, already dead. When Noodles first returns to the Lower East Side in 1968, he watches a backhoe lifting a gravestone out of the ground: the Jewish cemetery in being dug up (and, as he learns, his friends' bodies have been moved to their mausoleum in Riverdale). These are just the first suggestions of death and resurrection, contrasting Noodles and Max (Noodles has been 'dead' while living for the past 35 years while Max has been living while 'dead').

Max's betrayal of Noodles is foreshadowed as a form of death throughout the film: as when Noodles asks him what he would do if Menaldi asked one of them to kill the other; it is made more specific when the politician Sharkey tells Max that Noodles is 'dead weight.' This recalls Noodles' invention which saves the crates of liquor thrown overboard, which sink to the bottom and rise to the surface: remember that the first time the boys recover the crates, Max falls in the water and plays dead, while Noodles searches for him in panic. When Noodles finally confronts Deborah backstage and she warns him not to go through the door (where he will see David), he asks if he will turn into a pillar of salt. Salt was the device Noodles used to weight the sunken crates.

While Noodles was in prison, Max got the gang a legitimate business cover as undertakers, 'grave-robbers' as he calls it. He meets Noodles at the prison gates with a 'dead' woman who miraculously comes back to life. And the night Noodles betrays Max is punctuated by the end of Prohibition, announced by a coffin brought into Fat Moe's.

Triangles: Rather than a triangular battle between main characters, as in his Westerns, Leone here uses triangles to map out the love relationships. The most obvious involves Noodles' love life: Fat Moe's love for Noodles is as unquestioning as Deborah's is restrained by her own self-interest. More crucially, Leone actually tells the film's main love story, that of Max and Noodles, by a series of constantly changing triangles.

Twice Noodles will triangulate women with himself and Max. He assumes he is the reason Max and Deborah hate each other so much, an assumption which will be used against him by Max, through Carol, who tells Noodles they don't like each other before asking his help in betraying Max.

According to Elizabeth McGovern, Leone saw the Max/Noodles relationship as a "failed love affair." She told Frayling she felt it didn't work because it wasn't "sexy" enough, largely because of De Niro's restraint in performance. Certainly James Woods' combination of leering jealous looks and suggestive cigar-sucking gets the point across; Woods always seems jealous of the women with Noodles, rather than of Noodles himself.

In the film, Max is paired with three women. In all three cases he has the women after Noodles: immediately in the case of Peggy, shortly afterwards with Carol and years later with Deborah. When Carol first 'claims' him, she also reaches to Noodles, trying to entice him into a threesome (and then a foursome, which foreshadows Max's eventual relationship with Deborah). Noodles' response is "Besides, I'm afraid if I gave you a good crack in the mouth you'd probably like it," an interesting bit of double entendre, which also prefigures Deborah's rape.

The Rapes: The last time I saw *Once Upon A Time In America* in a cinema, the woman with me left at the interval, which immediately followed the rape of Deborah. Both rape scenes are harsh, although the first, of Carol during the robbery, is more straightforward in its elements of masculine fantasy: Carol invites and enjoys the rough sex, and this quality has been set up by the story which Joe tells about her, being pimped by her insurance-salesman husband who offers Joe 'cock insurance', and is then followed up by scenes which show Carol's relative degree of control of her own sexuality.

Noodles' rape of Deborah is a different matter, particularly because he has been presented somewhat sympathetically in regard to her throughout the film. But that sympathy is one which requires the audience to ignore Noodles' basic nature as they warm to him as the 'hero' of the film. Noodles, like his friends, is a child of the streets and although he has his sensitive impulses, he doesn't know what to make of them. This is pointed out by the constant references to 'getting it up the ass' as the metaphor for beating someone at any aspect of the game. The young Noodles has his dream of romance, as evidenced by his reading *Martin Eden* in the privacy of the loo, but he also sees the reality of the streets, as his reading is interrupted by Peggy. The Madonna/whore dichotomy is rarely defined so clearly.

It is also reinforced just before Noodles rapes Deborah. He picks her up immediately after the scene in which Carol toys with the four friends before picking Max (going from the whores to the Madonna), and it is reinforced further by the visual images of Long Island which suggest *The Great Gatsby*, where Jay Gatz longs for his all-American Princess.

The young Noodles also foreshadows the rape. In the first shift to 1922, which comes as the aged Noodles looks through the peephole where he once watched Deborah dancing, we hear him telling his friends "If she don't leave me alone I'm gonna give her what she's asking for." Deborah isn't the one who won't leave Noodles alone - it's the other way around. And just as tellingly, it's not until she actually does tell him she's leaving him alone that he does give her what she hasn't been asking for.

Deborah is a classic Jewish American Princess, particularly in her younger Jennifer Connolly incarnation. She refuses to help in the family restaurant, she receives dancing, elocution and French lessons, and she treats Noodles with a mixture of love tempered by the knowledge that he will never measure up to her standards. This too will be reinforced in the adult Deborah, who reminds Noodles that his life is his choice.

To put the rape in context, we have to remember Noodles telling Deborah the two things he thought about in prison were Dominic's last words ("I slipped") and her, but he doesn't appear to have made the leap to admit that he has slipped as well. He quotes 'Song Of Songs' back to Deborah, his first consciously romantic gesture, and it is at that point she tells him she is leaving for Hollywood.

In the car we get the film's most powerful moment: first we watch a cold screen descend over De Niro's face as he recoils like a powerful adolescent from the blow received when he opened himself, and then McGovern's kiss, which I see as compassionate, but which Adrian Martin describes, just as convincingly, as 'condescending.' Certainly McGovern, not terribly convincing as a Jap, is extremely convincing in her vulnerability, her mix of shock and fear, her pain at Noodles' betrayal when he rapes her. Her wit cannot match the power of Noodles' anger, and McGovern conveys all those emotions superbly.

The rape is presented without humorous dialogue to lessen the pain, as it was in Carol's scene, there is no music on the soundtrack, just the harsh mocking sound of seagulls. It is a painful scene to watch and this is as it should be. We share the chauffeur's contempt of Noodles, but this would have been emphasised even more by a scene cut from the film, where Noodles talks to the chauffeur while waiting for Deborah outside the theatre (the scenes of Deborah's dancing were also cut). The chauffeur, played by producer Arnon Milchan, is an early Jewish refugee from Germany, and he tells Noodles that the Jewish gangsters are not looked up to in the community, the way Mafiosi may be in the Italian community. This reminds us of the violent course Noodles has chosen, just as Deborah reminded Noodles earlier that it is, indeed, his choice.

Yet we also feel some pity for Noodles' inability to understand either Deborah or himself. The point will be reinforced in 1968, when Noodles realises that Deborah, who rejected him as a two-bit hood, has been Max's lover, presumably once he became a business and political figure as successful as she was in her career. If Deborah's affection for Noodles confuses him, it may also confuse us. After all, though she admits she might like a life with Noodles, and clearly is attracted to him, she constantly leavens her affection. She taunts him as children, she leaves him bleeding in the alley and she somewhat coldly rejects him at the moment he makes himself most vulnerable. This is not to excuse his actions, but to put into the context that cold screen which descends on De Niro's features.

In 1968, when Noodles tells her that, having seen her act as Cleopatra (again, the actual performance was cut from the film) he knows she made the right decision in choosing her career over him, she almost immediately loses her ability to act, unable to either explain the truth to Noodles, or convince him to abandon his quest. Noodles will not realise just how shattered his last illusion is until the instant he sees David standing outside.

Leone neither condones nor glamorises the rape. But in his cinema of male relations, it is seen first as an expression of Noodles' character. Up until that point Noodles had kept Deborah separate from the boy-gangster world of violence, force and instant gratification, but in the back seat of the car he first shuts himself off to her. Then, when she makes a gesture to draw him back to the closeness they knew, he reacts as he would to any gesture of weakness from an outsider. In *The Rise And Fall Of Legs Diamond* Alice tells Legs "as long as someone loved you, you were OK." Noodles loses Deborah's love, and from that point his life begins its inexorable slide downhill. It is a powerful and disturbing piece of film-making.

He Can Shoot, Too: Cockeye playing the pan pipes, echoing Harmonica's harmonica, was drawn directly from Grey's novel, only in the book Cockeye actually did play the harmonica!

The March Of Time: Just as Dominic, while dying, says "I slipped," so Max and Noodles both slip in and out of time - both in figurative deaths, as noted above, and literally within the flashback structure of the film. This is echoed in the pocket watch motif and in the key to the locker, the key to the whole mystery, being kept in Fat Moe's grandfather clock, one of many in the bar.

This sense of recovering the past, discovering lost memory, echoes Orson Welles in his first two films. When Noodles confronts Carol, in the Bailey Foundation, Leone gives us the most poignant visual echo of *Citizen Kane* (1941). Noodles has been playing the Jed Leland character who retraces a biography (crucially, his own, as well as Max's) by interviewing people from the past. The sense of a lost past is recalled in shots which echo the George and Fanny staircase scene and the beautiful close-up of Major Amberson in *The Magnificent Ambersons* (1942).

Bad News For Jennifer Connelly Internet Freaks: If anything, Connelly is more effective as young Deborah than McGovern is as the adult, and at times she seems even more adult. But her nude scenes were body-doubled by Margherita Pace, and as far as I know, no websites devoted to Margherita Pace exist.

The Verdict: Great art, as John Keats said, has to exist in mystery, confusion and doubt. Some critics are bothered by the ambiguities of *Once Upon A Time In America*. I'm not. Perversely though, I think the readdition of one or two of the cut sequences would improve it. Even so, Leone's first venture outside the western since 1960 is a masterpiece. 5/5

Leone's Last War

Leone spent much of the last five years of his life trying to raise the money for a film based on the siege of Leningrad. He'd conceived the idea in 1969, based on hearing Shostakovich's 7th Symphony, and it had been reborn when he read Harrison Salisbury's best-seller, *The 900 Days*. Although no script ever existed, Leone had raised nearly a third of a proposed $50 million budget, which would have been done as the first ever co-production with the Soviet film industry. Although various screenwriters names were bandied about, no screenplay ever existed.

During this time he became a Wellesian figure, both because of his expanding girth and his expansive delight in projects that would never be realised (both men were fascinated by the Don Quixote tale; Leone's was to have been set in modern America). He continued to direct commercials; unlike Welles, he never acted in them. He remained devoted to his cinematic heroes, writing appreciations of John Ford and Charlie Chaplin for Italian newspapers.

He worked with Sergio Donati on a TV mini-series project called *The Gun*, which would follow one gun's progress from person to person. He also worked up, with Luca Morsella and Fabio Toncelli, a screenplay intended for Mickey Rourke and Richard Gere, which Morsella, the son of Leone's producer Fulvio, would direct. Called *A Place Only Mary Knows*, it is a Civil War story with strong overtones of *The Good, The Bad And The Ugly*.

In January 1989 he filmed a Renault 19 commercial in Zimbabwe, the car on a rope bridge. He came back from Zimbabwe in February and went to Moscow where final agreements were apparently close to being completed on his Leningrad film. On 30 April 1989, he and his wife Carla sat in bed watching Susan Hayward in Robert Wise's *I Want To Live* (1958). His heart simply stopped beating and he died. At the funeral, Ennio Morricone played the main theme from *Once Upon A Time In The West* on the church organ.

Leone's Legacy

Leone lives on today as one of the most influential directors of his time. Every time we hear the argument about Quentin Tarantino 'lifting' his face-to-face confrontations from Ringo Lam, we should be thinking about Leone. He has been influential in ways he never could have imagined, as his stylised violence, amoral characters, cynical world-view have become commonplace, and his use of close-ups, of music, of pacing and ritual are today clichés.

His influence is seen everywhere from Tsui Hark's homage in *Once Upon A Time In China* (1992) to the Westerns showing in the background of *The Harder They Come* (1973). Leone's work exerts an influence well beyond that of the Western. Today film-makers quote his scenes the same way Leone quoted the directors he admired.

Often they do it consciously, with a knowing wink to the audience, implying that Leone's work is so well known as to have been assimilated into the myths it portrayed. Just as Leone's West was derived from the movies of his youth, much of our present day cinema of violence comes directly from Leone.

Plus he has contributed to the language of cinema, and his use of setting, editing, close-ups and music are everywhere. Leone didn't discover Ennio Morricone, but it was their collaboration that put Morricone on the map. Leone did, in a fashion, discover Clint Eastwood, who has grown into one of the major directors of the past quarter century.

It is a giant legacy for a man who directed only seven films. Yet four of those seven deserve the highest ratings which they have received in this study, and that is a success rate few directors could achieve. As noted, in his later years he was often compared in personality to Welles. Yet their career paths were diametrically opposite. Leone's progress was a gradual education, completely within directing cinema, and it took him years before he reached the point where, like Welles, the business of achieving what he wanted seemed to become too much. We look back on his unrealised projects with the same feeling of loss. What would we give for more films from Leone, but how grateful we are for the ones we have.

Resource Materials

Videos & DVDs

A Fistful of Dollars (MGM/UA) DVD 16169, VHS 16169S, VHS Widescreen 16169W

For A Few Dollars More (MGM/UA) DVD 16170, VHS 16170S, VHS Widescreen 16170W

The Good, The Bad And The Ugly (MGM/UA) DVD 15813, VHS 15813S, VHS Widescreen 15813W - The DVD version, like the VHS, has the four crucial sequences restored from the original UK release and also includes seven further clips omitted from the final cut, six of which are described in Frayling's *Spaghetti Westerns*.

These three are available in a box set called *Spaghetti Westerns* in all three formats (MGM/UA) 20682

Once Upon A Time In The West (Paramount) VHS BRP2997, VHS Widescreen VHR4197

Duck, You Sucker/A Fistful of Dynamite out of print

Once Upon A Time In America (Warner) VHS PES38145 (228-minute version)

Sergio Leone

Sergio Leone: Something To Do With Death by Christopher Frayling (Faber & Faber, 2000) No one writing about Leone can fail to acknowledge the enormous debt we owe Professor Frayling for his biography, an epic of research and scholarship. I have drawn heavily on his book for biographical details and background in the Italian cinema, as well as depended on it as the ultimate arbiter of accuracy when facts are in doubt. Any inaccuracies, in this volume, of course, are my own. Beyond that debt, however, I cannot emphasise too strongly that if you have any serious interest in Leone, or if this book has prompted some, Frayling's book is a must-read. In fact, the only must-read on the list. It's comprehensive, thoughtful, analytical and thorough (in fact, dispiriting when one sees one's own insights pre-empted in print!) and despite its size, written in a casual enough tone (dotted with the odd eye-rolling pun: films that are "run of DeMille" or muscle epics "pumping irony") to make it a consistently engrossing read.

Sergio Leone: The Great Italian Dream Of Legendary America by Oreste De Fornari (Gremese International 1997, Original Edition 1984) This study, translated into English, is almost as valuable as Frayling's, but one sometimes has to take the Leone interviews with a grain of salt, as Frayling's book shows. The introductory essay by Luc Mollet is concise and brilliant, De Fornari's own analyses are interesting, and there are a dozen revealing interviews with Leone's collaborators and contemporaries which are invaluable. It is comprehensively illustrated.

Once Upon A Time In America by Adrian Martin (BFI Modern Classics, 1999) Martin's single film study is one of the best in this series, in fact, one of the few of the modern series which ranks with the excellent Film Classics series. Martin is a sensitive critic, and like Leone's film itself, moves back and forth in time and space to present a compelling picture of a great film.

Viva Leone! A BBC documentary produced in 1989 by Nick Freund Jones, this follows Christopher Frayling's research, and Frayling is the major talking head, but also features interview material with Leone, Morricone, Valerii, Henry Fonda and Alex Cox.

Once Upon A Time: The Films Of Sergio Leone by Robert Cumbow (Scarecrow Press, 1987)

On the web, there are a number of Leone sites which feature photos but little information. The exception is the Sergio Leone Homepage (http://film.tierranet.com/directors/s.leone/sergioleone.html) Produced by Leone fan extraordinaire Cenk Kiral, its highlight is a series of interviews by Kiral with Sergio Donati, Luciano Vincenzoni, Mickey Knox and Christopher Frayling.

Spaghetti Westerns

Spaghetti Westerns by Christopher Frayling (IB Tauris 1999, Original Edition 1981) As if the definitive Leone biography were not enough, Frayling also published, twenty years ago, the best study of the Spaghetti Western so far. His emphasis here too is with Leone, including detailed analysis of many of his influences, both American and Italian, which is not repeated in the biography. The new edition is presented attractively.

Italian Western: The Opera Of Violence by Laurence Staig and Tony Williams (Lorrimer, 1975) Long out of print, this early study has a separate chapter on Leone and focuses on the stylistic aspects of the genre. It's a little chaotic, but it's lively and well illustrated, and if you ever see a copy on a shelf somewhere, snatch it up.

Spaghetti Westerns by Howard Hughes (Pocket Essentials, 2001) Like the present volume, a quick overview. Hughes defines and charts the Spaghetti genre quickly and effectively, then gives credits, synopses and analysis of thirty-one representative films. A nice companion piece to this volume.

L'America A Roma, a 1998 RAI documentary directed by Gianfranco Pannone, which features the reminiscences of Guglielmo Spoletini, a stuntman and actor in Spaghetti Westerns (as William Bogart) and some of his colleagues from the glory days of Cinecittà.

Westerns

Horizons West by Jim Kitses (Indiana University Press, 1970) The classic analysis of Anthony Mann, Budd Boetticher and Sam Peckinpah, a must-read for anyone interested in Westerns.

Gunfighter Nation by Richard Slotkin (Athaneum, 1992) The third volume of Slotkin's monumental study of the myth of the American frontier, it is packed with insight on Western literature and film.

Wild West Movies by Kim Newman (Bloomsbury, 1990) A thematically-organised study informed by Newman's always sharp vision and writing style.

The BFI Companion To The Western ed by Edward Buscombe (MOMI 1991, Original Edition 1988) An essential reference work for any Western fan.

The Western ed by Phil Hardy (Aurum Film Encyclopedias 1991, Original Edition 1983) Useful for its year-by-year rundowns. Calls *A Fistful Of Dollars* 'the most influential Western of the decade (1960s).'

Movie Book Of The Western ed by Ian Cameron & Douglas Pye (Studio Vista/Cassell, 1996).

The Western Reader ed by Jim Kitses & Gregg Rickman (Limelight Editions, 1998) More interesting for its takes on classic Westerns and on feminist Westerns of the 1990s than its sole essay on Leone.

Westerns: Making The Man In Fiction And Film by Lee Clark Mitchell (Univ of Chicago, 1996) Includes a well-argued chapter on Leone and Peckinpah 'turning the genre inside out.'

The Crowded Parade: American National Identity In The Hollywood Western by Michael Coyne (IB Tauris, 1997).

Among individual director studies I'd particularly recommend *Anthony Mann* by Jeanine Basinger (Twayne, 1979), *Samuel Fuller* by Nicholas Garnham (Viking, 1972), *Samuel Fuller* by Phil Hardy (Studio Vista, 1970), *John Ford* by Peter Bogdanovich (Univ of California, revised edition 1978) and the volumes on *Stagecoach* and *The Searchers* by Edward Buscombe, and *High Noon* by Philip Drummond in the BFI Film Classics series.

Articles:

'Once Upon A Time In Italy' Stuart M Kaminsky, *The Velvet Light Trap* 12, 1974

'Johnny Guitar' Michael Wilmington, *The Velvet Light Trap* 12, 1974

'Killing Time' Geoffrey O'Brien, *New York Review Of Books*, 3 March 1992

'A Fable For Adults' interview with Leone by Elaine Lomenzo, *Film Comment*, August 1984

'Once Upon A Time' Mary Corliss, *Film Comment*, August 1984

'Something To Do With Death' Richard T Jameson, *Film Comment*, March 1983

'Once Upon A Time In Italy' David Nicholls, *Sight & Sound*, Winter 1980/81

'Once Upon A Time In America' Tony Rayns, *Monthly Film Bulletin*, October 1984

'Worth A Few Dollars More' Edward Buscombe, *Sight & Sound*, January 2001

'Strength Of Character: Eli Wallach' Michael Billington, *The Guardian*, 24 July 2000

Clint Eastwood

My favourite Eastwood biography remains Stuart Kaminsky's (yes, the same guy who scripted *Once Upon A Time In America) Clint Eastwood* (Signet Books, 1974) mostly because it is so straightforward and lacks the benefit of hindsight and import under which studies like this one labour. The most complete Eastwood biography is Richard Schickel's *Clint Eastwood* (1997), which is, in effect, the authorised version and benefits from Schickel's critical acumen. It stops short of hagiography, but if you crave the seamier tabloid side of Eastwood's life, try Patrick McGilligan's *Clint's World* (1999). There are literally hundreds of articles and interviews available on Eastwood, the only one cited directly here was Dick Lochte's from the Los Angeles Free Press, 20 April 1973. Like Kaminsky's book, it has a certain freshness (and like Kaminsky, Lochte became a successful crime novelist). I used two documentaries: the 1995 ITV *South Bank Show* produced by Gerald Fox and the 2000 BBC *Arena* two-parter produced by Bruce Ricker and Dave Kehr for PBS's American Playhouse. The latter is more informative, with extensive interviewing of his collaborators and others, including Martin Scorsese and Richard Slotkin.

Ennio Morricone

Two websites in English are particularly useful. A short biography and a first-rate Cineaste interview can be found at (http://lavender.fortunecity.com/pulpfiction/348). A complete filmography is at Movie Music UK (www.shef.ac.uk/~cm1jwb/morricone.htm).

The Essential Library

New This Month:

Sergio Leone (£3.99)   **Spaghetti Westerns** (£3.99)
Nietzsche (£3.99)   **David Lynch** (£3.99)
Film Noir (£3.99)

New Next Month:

Steven Spielberg (£3.99)   **Feminism** (£3.99)
Sherlock Holmes (£3.99)   **Alchemists & Alchemy** (£3.99)

Film Directors:

Jane Campion (£2.99)   **John Carpenter** (£3.99)
Jackie Chan (£2.99)   **Joel & Ethan Coen** (£3.99)
David Cronenberg (£3.99)   **Terry Gilliam** (£2.99)
Alfred Hitchcock (£2.99)   **Krzysztof Kieslowski** (£2.99)
Stanley Kubrick (£2.99)   **David Lynch** (£3.99)
Brian De Palma (£2.99)   **Sam Peckinpah** (£2.99)
Ridley Scott (£3.99)   **Orson Welles** (£2.99)
Billy Wilder (£3.99)   **Woody Allen** (£3.99)

Film Genres:

Heroic Bloodshed (£2.99)   **Horror Films** (£3.99)
Slasher Movies (£3.99)   **Vampire Films** (£2.99)

Miscellaneous Film Subjects:

Steve McQueen (£2.99)   **Marilyn Monroe** (£3.99)
The Oscars® (£3.99)   **Filming On A Microbudget** (£3.99)

TV:

Doctor Who (£3.99)

Books:

Cyberpunk (£3.99)   **Philip K Dick** (£3.99)
Hitchhiker's Guide (£3.99)   **Noir Fiction** (£2.99)
Terry Pratchett (£3.99)

Ideas:

Conspiracy Theories (£3.99)

Available at all good bookstores, or send a cheque to: **Pocket Essentials (Dept SL), 18 Coleswood Rd, Harpenden, Herts, AL5 1EQ, UK**. Please make cheques payable to 'Oldcastle Books.' Add 50p postage & packing for each book in the UK and £1 elsewhere.

US customers can send $6.95 plus $1.95 postage & packing for each book to: **Trafalgar Square Publishing, PO Box 257, Howe Hill Road, North Pomfret, Vermont 05053, USA**. e-mail: tsquare@sover.net

Customers worldwide can order online at **www.pocketessentials.com**.